Perfect Imperfection

Poems by

James D. Rapp

~

Introduction

If it is worth doing, it is worth doing poorly.

Many years ago I attended a Mock United Nations with a group of high school students from the school where I was teaching. The students and their advisors were divided into workgroups for some of the early preliminary exercises and required to report to the entire assembly the results of their group's work. We were all amused when one group, apparently feeling that the product of their efforts didn't measure up with that of the other groups, prefaced their presentation with the announcement that they had adopted the principle: "If it is worth doing, it is worth doing poorly."

Obviously, a counterintuitive notion. But upon reflection, and correctly understood, it makes sense. Not everyone has the skill to build a perfect house, but if the crying need is for a house to be build it is better to build it "poorly" than to stay exposed to the elements. So it is with many other, less urgent, tasks.

I have mentioned elsewhere in this book that a teacher once told our high school class of sophomore English students that the definition of poetry was: "the best use of the best words." If I have found the best words, and used them well, this volume needs no caveat to justify its printing. In those instances in which I have failed, I too will claim the right to do "poorly" that which, nonetheless, my heart has told me is worth doing.

James Rapp

Contents

Introduction i

Seeing The World 1

Me and God (And Some Farmer) 3
Thoughts About A Misty Monday Morning 4
Rain 5
Close Pleasures 6
Storms 6
Seeing the World 7
Tricky Autumn 7
Spellbound 8

Astigmatism 9

Autonomy: To Be Or Not To Be 11
The Longest Word 11
A Seminal Question 12
Congenital Twins 12
Tea-peed 12
Consistency 13
A Weatherman's Lot Is Not A Happy One 13
On Naming 14
Ducky Days 15
Period . . . *italicized* 16
Astigmatism 17
Twinkle Toes 18
A Play Without A Script 19
Incorrectly Rectal 19
Upon Being Appointed *Lever Laureate* 20
Planning for the Future 20
A Sea-sick Mariner's Lament 21
The Parent's Tithe 21
The River From Lothlorien 22
A Little Comfort For An Untidy Man 22
A Sabbath Remembered 23
Superlatives 24
Unlinked Hours 25

No Animals Died 26
Less Les 27
Some Things I'd Rather Not Know 28

The Mystery of Luminosity 31

Luna 33
Faithful Luna 33
Our Luna Friend 34
Luna on a Cold, Cold, Night 34
Come! Enjoy the Moon! 34
A Joy Worth Waking For 35
Naked Reflection 36
Luna and Sol 37
Eclipsed 38
The Mystery of Luminosity 38
Making Mud Into Moonlight 39
An Invitation to Dance: Declined 39
An Eye Opener 40
Sol Rising 41

Concentrated Light 43

Perfect Imperfection 45
Not My Words, But Thine 46
Concentrated Light 47
Heart Work 47
The Best Use Of The Best Words 48
Introspection 49
Truth Tellers 50
On Sources of Inspiration 51
The Meaning of Silence 52
Praise 53
Wonderful Memories 53
The Poet's Sword 54
A Resolution From A Very Wordy Man 54
What Is A Poem? 55
As You Have Said, Let It Be Unto Me 55
On Reviewing My Poetry 57

What Mean These Stones? 59

   In Memoriam 61
   Honor 61
   A Mother's Day Poem for My Wife 62
   What We Know About Friendship............................ 62
   An Ode To Three Wonderful Boys 64
   What Mean These Stones.. 65
   A "Song" for Bud & Pat 66
   A Valentine Poem 67
   A Valentine's Day Poem 68
   A Valentine's Day Prayer 68
   For A Nurse-Friend Watching Her Father Die.......... 69
   The Matriculation of a Young Lady 70
   In Memory of Sylvia – A Dear Friend 71
   Father of fathers 71
   Thank You, Ruth and Arlene 72
   A Cup of Warm II 73
   To Allison 74
   A Birthday Blessing.. 74
   The "Story" of Dan 75
   A Wish For Joy 76
   A Pastor 76
   The Renaming of Jacob 77
   On Loving (or not) The Wrinkles 79
   Two Rocks 79

The Prophet's Eye 81

   The Prophet's Eye... 83
   A Work Deferred For Lack of Purity 85
   Truth 86
   Thinking About Man's Use of Time 87
   The Danger of "Knowing" The Truth 87
   A Prayer For Peace 88
   Justice 88
   Living In The Shadow of a Shadow 90
   On Faithfulness 91
   Righteousness 91
   More Questions Than Time Allows.......................... 92

Heel Pullers 94
A Prayer For My Neighbor 95
Mortality 95
Countless Shades 96
A Hill Far-away 97
Balaam's Speaking Ass 98
Men Who Know What They Know 99
A Patriot's Prayer and a Response 100
Ahasuerus's Sin 100
Love By Demolition 101
Supernova (The Lonely Center) 102
Mixed Economies 104
On Being Right 105
Of Shepherds and Sheep 106
At the End of the World 109
Voice to Voice 110
A Defining Issue: What is Pentecostal? 111
Name Bearers 113
The Storm 114
Jehovah-Rapha 117
On Democracy 119
A Final Word 120
Forgiveness 122
This Is My Body 123
Pentecost 125
Parallel Lives: Inversely Related 125
Images 127
Redemption 128

Heart's Ease: The Home of Heart 131

What is the Shape of Joy? 133
Morning's Soft Light 133
Psalm 99 134
I'll Rise on His Love 134
Sharing Joy 135
Sunday Morning "Him" Singing 136
Heart's Ease: The Home of Heart 136
A Prayer for June 3, 2005 136
The Servant's Prayer 137

A Hymn	139
A Prayer for Friday, February 11, 2005	140
The Perfect Day	141
You Are Joy!	141
A Samaritan Leper's Song	142
Good Morning!	143
In All Things Give Thanks	144
Four Words	144
Sunday Graces	145
How Will We Praise Him?	145
A Sunday Morning Prayer	145
Come Lord	146
Patience	146
Let Everything That Hath Breath Praise Him	147
The Gift of Time	147
A Prayer	148
Martha's Complaint	148
A Path to Joy	149
A Grain of Mustard Seed	150
Grace	153
A Sunday Morning Poem	154
Morning Hope	155
The Goal, The Way, and the Key	155
A Prayer for a Glorious Day	156
Good Morning Sunshine	156
A Triangle of Love	157
Preciousness	157
The Voice of God	158
Loose Ends	162
Looking on the Bright Side	163
Rumors of Eden	**165**
Phenomena	167
Pleasure Seeking	167
I Must Go	168
A Child's Gift of Love	169
Defining Beauty	170
The Teacher's Burden	170
A Lament at the End of the Day	171

Waking Thoughts 172
Something 172
The Worth of a Touch 172
Shadowed Blessings 173
Sin 173
A Lament for Atheists 174
Friendship.. 174
A Malleable Moment 176
Rumors of Eden... 177
Because You Asked 178
Last Thoughts.. 179
Time-Tied... 179
Recognizing God's Goodness 180
A Cup of Warm 180
If I Could 180
On Being Perfect 181
Troubled Waters 181
Wednesdays Ending 182
Not Hearing Less... 183
Love Is Not Blind.. 184
Daring a Correction 185
Four Healings 186
A Prayer for Selflessness... 186
Precious Gift of Life.. 187
The Eternal Day 187
Morning's Message 188
The Making of Ezer... 188
Seeking A Mate And Finding One's Self.......................... 189
The Prayer of Hezekiah 190
Trail's End.. 190
An Ode to Memory 191
On A Gloomy Morning 192
Continental Drift 193

A Divine Mystery.. 195

Snowflakes 197
An Old-fashioned Christmas 197
Mary and Joseph in the Shadowlands 198
One Clear Star 200

The Peace Maker	200
A Child's Way	201
The Postage Is So High	201
He Didn't Come To Be A Star	202
One Clear Star	203
This Is Christmas	204
A Divine Mystery	205
Alphabetical List of Poems	207

x

Seeing The World

We are shaped and nourished by the world in which we live, its physical, social, emotional, economic and political climate. But more than those, we are influenced by the specific people who occupy that world with us. Forrest and B. J. Lovett have, for the last many years, enriched our lives as we have explored many parts of our world together, some far away, but most closer at hand. Forrest was instrumental in instigating our wonderful "Group of Six Tours", beginning with the unforgettable "Roots Tours." The time spent enjoying good company and seeing the world around us is a gift of inestimable worth.

To Forrest and B.J. I dedicate this first section of poems.

Me and God (And Some Farmer)

I own a beautiful little meadow
        that lies off to the right of the highway
        about a quarter of the way
        between home and work.
Well, it might be more accurate
        to say that I own it, in partnership,
        with God who made it,
        and some unknown farmer,
        who undoubtedly makes the payments.

But I suppose God is the major partner.
He has done,
        and continues to do,
        most of the work.
He threaded Otter Creek through its grassy lowlands.
In the spring he greens up the grass and trees
        and sends an army of underground critters
        to hump up its surface.
All summer long it lies like an undiscovered park,
        cool and inviting.
And, each autumn, He spreads it over
        with the glorious colors of Fall.

But this morning was the best of all.
He filled my meadow with a low-lying, frosty fog
        that obscured everything
        but the tops of the surrounding hills.
My heart skipped, and I cried, "Thank you God!"

I must remember to be grateful for the work my partners do –
        to God for His creative skills,
        and the farmer for the payments.
They owe me nothing – mine is a labor of love.

Thoughts About A Misty Monday Morning

What would ever make
one insensitive
to a fog enshrouded,
dawning day like this?

She would have to lose
awareness of the smells
that hang upon the heavy air;
that bear the essence of grass,
and tree, and bush.
And she would have to lose
the sense her skin can feel
as dewdrops form upon her cheeks.

He would have to turn
deaf ears to the call of bird,
or sound of trickling water,
or the gentle creak of swings
moving in the breeze.

Blind, they'd need to be,
to the elven shapes,
formed by fog and early light;
the frosted, muted shapes
that, in full light, will be
the ordinary things of daily life.

They would have to sear
their tongues;
to dull the taste
of morning freshness --
the taste of life --
in the air they breath.

Oh, sister, brother, friend,
may all Monday mornings
bring our praise to Him
who formed the earth,
and set it in a sphere of time,
dividing that in sevens,
and filling each with evidence
of His great power --
of His great love --
that covers earth
and fills the heavens.

Rain

Rain is not a bother
If you think about it as a gift
From our loving father,
And, instead of grumbling, praises lift.

Is there really anything,
Ill, or well received,
That His sheltering wing
Cannot over-eave?

I stand beneath His eaves
And watch the falling rain;
Know the richness it achieves,
And praise His goodness once again.

Close Pleasures

For being such a "stick in the mud"
I've actually been to a lot of places;
Some of which I still, with pleasure, laud
And some have hardly left their traces.

Nine different nations I've seen,
And nearly every state of the union.
I've traveled both heavy and lean -
Lean is best in my humble opinion.

But the best places aren't far away;
To reach them takes less than a day;
They're the paths that are hidden from view;
Places surprisingly pleasant and new.

But a pause in our new-place-seeking-quest
Will reveal, close at hand, the best of the best;
Beauties residing in nature and friend,
In the sound of the wind . . . or the touch of a hand.

Storms

Storms have always made me glad.
Half weather cock, I've always had
My "vane" turned to catch the wind
That brings the next nor'easter in.
Rain can seldom come too hard,
Snow drifts need no calling card;
Lightning bolts and thunder claps,
Wind that pushes water into "caps",
Waves the treetops to and fro,

And buries things in foot-deep snow,
Are friends that bring much joy to me,
Stirring up a world become too sendentry,
Or slowing one that spins frenetically.

Seeing The World

It doesn't require a visa or passport
To see the world around you.
Today I've watched a sky full of clouds sport,
Filling the heavens from some westward port,
Whirling in forms ever new,
Spreading as though their darkness could thwart
The sunshine and cover the blue.
And well their rowdy cavort,
With the wind at their backs for support,
May give them a "victory" or two,
But the sun is coming with his glorious consorts;
Surrounded indeed by a cloud escort,
Riding the heavens in his chariot of blue.

Tricky Autumn

There is no season like autumn.
Its warm colors slowly come,
Branch by branch, tree by tree,
Until one day they are upon us
In a flare of golds and reds and green.

Carpet and canopy bracket our days
In a cacophony of colors that stay
Only long enough to tease our hearts
Into believing that there's no way
That winter could be just two months away.

Spellbound

They say it will snow tonight.
Familiar things, removed from sight –
Mere mounds of varying heights –
Enchant the wanderer's awe-struck sight.

One can be lost in such a storm.
Losing points of reference, torn
From one reality and not yet born
Into the next, one wanders thus forlorn.

Deceptively the snow enfolds
And whispers gently, to the one it holds,
A tale, a lie, too often told
To those it murders with its cold.

They say it will snow tonight,
And all the snowflakes, frail and white,
Join in luring, with their might,
A victim, spellbound by their awesome sight.

Astigmatism

Many things influence the way we see the world but none more wonderfully that the eyes of children. Alice and I have been allowed to see the world though the eyes of three wonderful children, Michelle Dawn (Shelly), Shawn David, and Cheryl Diane (Cheri). They should not have to bear the blame for the quirky ways I sometimes see things – my "astigmatism" – but they have frequently helped to liberate me from the bondage of adult perceptions. That is a gift, more precious the older we get, more necessary if we are to maintain a fresh view of our world.

And so I dedicate this section of poems to our dear children with thanks for all the love and joy they have brought into our lives.

Autonomy: To Be Or Not To Be

What if every atom in me
Insisted on autonomy?
And what if each desired to be
Something utterly,
Utterly, otherly?
Soon I'd be
Less than what I used to be.
And eventually . . .
Non-entity!
I'd cease to be!

Is there a lesson here to see?
Perhaps a trillion atoms, floating free,
Could be more than each,
Alone, could ever hope to be.
By lending individuality
In service of some greater corporality,
They could be,
I venture cautiously,
A part of something quite observably
Close to being me.

The Longest Word
(After hearing grandsons argue about it.)

Some say the longest word in all the world
Is "ultraphotomicroscopicsilicovulcanokoniosis."
Others, prone with that to quarrel,
Avow its "supercalafragilisticexpialadotious."
I'm contending that the longest word;
Reaching from the highest heaven above,
To earth, and then to heaven again, backward,
Is the tiny, mighty, everlasting, never-ending, "Love."

A Seminal Question

Do tiny sperm, and little ovum,
In some way in microcosm,
Recapitulate their makers' spasms,
Defeat all odds, and have orgasms,
As they romp in protoplasm?

Congenital Twins
(An Ode To The Hands)

Twins, but not identical,
Mirror images actually,
Joined in purpose
Not in fact.
Equals but unequal,
Left serving right,
Right assisting left
Without strife
Without regret,
Finding union
By embracing
What divides.

Tea-peed
(A poem in response to a Web Shots E-card showing an electric lighted Tepee on the open prairie . Somehow the card got sent three times)

I've been tea-peed upon when I was very wee,
My brother slept with me;
He peed on me and I on he.

It may have been milk-pee we peed
And not pee made from tea,
But we were never rude enough to pee
      three tea-pees!

Consistency

I am the scourge of inconsistency!

Believing it to be the cement
Of all successful institutions,
I insist upon consistency, especially from
Those in places of responsibility.

Believing them to be the cement
That cements the cement
Of all successful institutions,
I hold them to a high,
Unflinching standard of righteousness.

And, to be true to my conviction,
I apply it rigorously to myself,
Graciously and *consistently*
Making grand and sweeping exceptions
To accommodate my many inconsistencies.

A Weatherman's Lot Is Not A Happy One

Rain in any form;
In raging storm
Or lazy trickle;
Helps to meet the norm

Proclaimed by fickle
Weathermen. Forlorn,
They're in an awful pickle
If it dawns, a sunny morn.

On Naming
(*Ish* and *Isha*)

A poetic wag was heard to muse,
"How odd that God should choose the Jews",
But that is not surprising; not half as odd
As that for which I'd like to query God.

I'd like to know just why he thought
The Hebrew tongue the thing that caught
The essence of the creatures of the earth;
The thing by which He'd designate the sexes, at their primal birth.

So "man" became, in Hebrew, *Ish*,
Pronounced as one would say, "I smell a fish",
And "woman", God called *Isha*, and just why,
Is hard to say, perhaps a temporary name – in-*isha*-ly.

But I'd not argue with our Maker;
Who'd surely say, "Leave her, friend, or take her,
But don't go whining over how she 'sounds'.
Just look and wonder at the way she makes her 'rounds'".

Detractors make of her a frilly lace,
Or set her worth upon her pretty face,
But God has set for her a harder place;
The one whose labor births the human race.

And when that labor's past, her work begins;
Changing diapers, wiping chins,
Providing life's essentials are her daily care;
Housing, food, and things to wear.

A special heart, God gave to her,
That binds her to her home, and stirs
In her a strong abiding care;
A fortress-love beyond compare.

Isha, God's gift to *Ish*,
His rib served back to him – a lovely dish;
From *Ish* she came, but then, for evermore,
Does *Ish* from *Isha* draw his daily store.

Ducky Days
(And unDucky Too)

There are days when life is good
And all our little duckies walk and swim
In flawless rows,
Executing every wish
And tracking, faithfully,
Our tos and fros.

But not all days are thusly blessed;
So on those other luckless ones
We curse and fret and rant
Because our duckies
Will not walk the line,
Or, even if they "will", they can't.

Lord help me know that ducky days,
Are gracious gifts from you,
And help me store a few of them,
In memory,
Against the time
When my duckies will not walk the line.

Period . . . *italicized.*
(More subtle than an exclamation point.)

Is it necessary to italicize the period?
Would anyone notice if I did?
This is not a joke, I'm deadly serious.
Periods thus demarked could rid
The world of ambiguity,
Subtly saying, but with all clarity,
"I say what I mean,
And mean what I say,
And this imperceptible rotation,
This slight tilting to the right,
Denotes conviction."

My mother practiced punctuation,
Italicizing, with her eyes,
A doubtful word or situation;
Raising one brow slightly
When she heard a word
That stirred her indignation;
Putting all on notice
Where she stood,
Subtly saying, without saying,
"I disapprove,
Period . . . italicized."

Astigmatism
(A poem for all my friends who share my affliction)

Look into the night sky
      and find a solitary star
            bright against the blackness.

Cover one eye and watch
      it leap a trillion miles
            in just a nano-second.

But when it knows that you have trained,
      once more, both eyes upon it,
            back it leaps, as though you wouldn't know.

You can smell the searing heat
      of its trajectory, forth and back,
            as it courses through the nothingness.

I wonder, did it have a family?
      Did it take them with it
            as it traveled to and fro?

Were any lost along the way
      Or burned to crisps in its
            trail of molten wantonness?

Did it try to calculate the cost,
      in stellar energy,
            of its impulsive leap?

Does it feel no guilt, no shame,
      that all those kilo-ergs that could have
            fed a trillion starving children

Were lost because it chose to "be a star"
        and show its speed and prowess
                in the blink of an eye?

Twinkle Toes

If we could choreograph our days
We'd have them never move in ways
That make us learn new steps
Or take us in beyond our depths.

No, we would play familiar songs
And dance in ways that we have long
Been trained to dance;
We'd seldom ever take a chance.

And when we did, we'd want to know
That there was something down below
To catch us if we fell;
So all we did would come out well.

But life is the great choreographer,
And only this we know for sure;
Each day will introduce a dance that's new;
And we will dance before it's through.

So why not choose this bright philosophy,
That God has sent this dance to me,
Or if not He, at least, of it, He knows,
And with His help I'll be a "twinkle toes".

A Play Without A Script

Have I ever penned words in praise
Of Saturday, penultimate of days?
Alas, Saturday, in all her varied ways
Is hard to capsulate in tidy lays.

For some, a day of lazing rest;
For others, travel is the best
Of ways to celebrate with zest
The seventh day, the day of rest.

A day to catch-it-up,
Or perhaps to ratchet up;
A day to clean it up,
Or exercise to lean it up.

Poor Saturday, so non-descript
That none can make its glory trip
With lightness o're the praising lip;
Alas, a play to play without a script.

Incorrectly Rectal

There was a doctor named Spitz
Who gave all his patients fits.
When his glove went rectal
They cursed him dialectal.
Spitz' practice is now on the fritz.

So be careful little hands what you do.

Upon Being Appointed *Lever Laureate*

I've just appointed myself poet laureate of 3405 Lever Street. Address me please as the Lever Laureate. Here is a sample of the work that got me the designation:

long lines and short
designating something
but what
fill the page
good thing the page isn't real
no trees died to feed this laureate's
insatiabilities only silicone from Iraqi deserts
and oil from Iranian wells
thoughts spill out and crowd together
intermingling their words creating puzzles
for great minds to solve
the last laugh is that of a laureate
carrying his $35,000 to the bank
and paying off a mere third of his
pathetic mortgage
hoping there will be a couple of
reappointments

Not bad when I look at it from a "critic's" point of view. It has balance, and rhythm, and an esthetic lack of structure. It could be more oblique but that takes practice and I am, after all, a relatively new laureate.

Planning for the Future

Old men sleep too much,
Their heads drooped down
Upon their chests

Or laid back upon the chair,
Their mouths drawn tight
Or open wide, emitting air.

I'm not old yet but now and then
I need to practice being so,
So when the day arrives
And I am forced to play the part
I'll know to fill the air with snores
Instead of other air-born darts.

A Sea-sick Mariner's Lament

I'm buried in a sea of debris,
Lost on the ocean wide;
It is easy for any and all to see
The mess I've been trying to hide.

How many pencils and pens do I need?
Of paper, how many stacks?
How many books that I've no time to read?
Or articles written by NYT hacks?

When I have the answer to questions like these
I'll have the sea by its tail;
I'll sail through its storms with practiced ease
For I'll have learned the meaning of "Bail!"

The Parent's Tithe

Parenting is a matter of nine to one --
Nine hugs for every scolding done,
Nine smiles for every off-tune song that's sung,
Nine praises, tripping from the tongue
For every volley from the critic flung.

You see, its tithing, standing on its head,
Giving nine good gifts instead
Of one -- seeing that the child is fed
With loving deeds that can be read
By heart, instead of head,
Before the child's own name she's said.

The River From Lothlorien

The river that runs from Lothlorien
To Hobbiton's humble nest,
Bears Elven wares in silver ships
That sail upon her crest,
And golden chests that over-flow
With treasures, small, to fill
A Hobbit's humble soul.
But best of all, among her store,
A letter in Elven script, and more,
An Elven broach that, aft and fore,
Bears the mark of an Elven Queen,
Galadriel, whose beauty, seen,
Forever marks the seer's heart;
Forever, and all the years between.

A Little Comfort For An Untidy Man

Life is an unsorted mess,
Isn't it?
Unsorted that, unsorted this . . .
We try to sort out things; to make them fit.

Astigmatism

Some seem to thrive
On unsorted-ness;
And their paychecks still arrive,
Adding clutter to the rest.

But some have found the clue
To ordered-ness;
Their desktops shine like new
In grand fastidiousness,

While some, like me,
Are buried still
In hopeless piles of old debris.
Enough, it is, to make one ill.

Life is an unsorted mess,
Isn't it?
Unsorted that; unsorted this . . .
And when we're done, it will all fit.

They'll gather all this sordid muck,
Unsorted though it be,
Put it in an automated truck,
And make it mulch to grow a tree.

A Sabbath Remembered

Sunday afternoons were meant to be
A time of quietness; an over-arching tree
That offered shade and beckoned me
To lie beneath its branches lazily.

Perfect Imperfection   Astigmatism

I remember times when Sundays
Were just such; we found a way
To slow the clock for half a day -
A lazy, restful Sabbath on us lay.

Ah, those were days idyllic,
When in our crowed little billet
We waited out the time and tried to fill it;
Counted down each lagging hour, with no good way to "kill it".

But boys will find a way somehow,
They'll practice "killing" on some cat or cow,
Or on a sibling if conditions will allow,
A "sacrificial Sabbath killing" - It was often *me* or *thou*.

Our Sabbaths aren't what they used to be,
We fill them, stem to stern, with "good" activity,
And miss the peaceful quiet that there used to be
When Sabbath meant a battle royal with my sibs and me.

Superlatives

Who invented superlatives,
And what purpose do they serve?
They make a broad assumption
That one thing is ultimate,
And declare it so with verve.

Of course One Thing is ultimate,
But really more "unlike" than best;
Can we really say that Father God
Is greater than those man-made gods?
Not "best", He is "unlike" the rest.

Perfect Imperfection Astigmatism

Who invented superlatives,
And what purpose do they serve?
When no two snowflakes are alike;
Both perfect in their form and purpose,
Who, to call one "best", would have the nerve?

It is my wicked heart that sorts and ranks,
And claims to know the best.
It wants to put the things it loves –
The things that serve its interests –
On the top and thus decrease the rest.

Oh Lord, help me to know the only best;
To see that all you make is good,
But understand you have a thousand wills –
That each is best for what it's made –
And make *my* best be what *You* would.

Unlinked Hours

I love it when . . .
No, I am amused at
Our reaction to
The news that
Things, long planned,
Have been postponed,
Or altogether scrubbed.

Perfect Imperfection   Astigmatism

I watch
As those who wisely choose
To change the course,
In deference to harms,
Well attested,
Find no harms attendant to
The things they now
Are free to do.

I agree.
I heartily agree,
And rush to do
Some thing the former plans
Would not permit me to.
Ah, happy choice
That breaks the chain
Of regimented days,
And gives, instead,
A dozen un-linked hours
That I can use in ways
My heart desires.

No Animals Died

A toasted tomato sandwich
Is a tasty way to scratch the itch
To be perfectly ecological,
Even vegan, earth grown, *au naturel*.

Whole grain pieces top and bottom
Spread thick with mayo, mustard on them.
Tomato, onion, lettuce, complete the core
Unless, of course, one thinks of something more.

But veggie, veggie, veggie is the goal,
No meats cooked on coals,
No sentient creature boiled, baked or fried,
No animal sacrificed.

With conscience clear the feast is laid.
The celebrants assemble, assured and staid,
A joy to share, unmarred they think, by mortality;
No thought, at this gay feast, of carnality.

Ah, to be oblivious! To not even know
That immigrant sweat once stained the tomato;
That farmers gave a precious year to grow the gain;
That the onions don't appear, except by human pain.

No human feast exists
That can't be called a Eucharist;
That echoes not the sacred one
In which the "flesh" we eat is God's own Son's.

"This is my body, broken for you,
This, in remembrance of me, you do."
Alas! No feast is set without a sacrifice,
Without the "giving" of *some* sacred life.

Less Les

Poor Tess,
       her heart a mess,
       had made the guess
       that more of Les
       increased her stress.

So in a fit of testiness,
        she more or less
        dismissed her lover, Les.
But now, alas,
        and loverless,
        she sees that Les
        has spotted Bess,
        and Bess is eyeing Les.
Poor Tess!
In sore distress,
        and ruing hastiness,
        she now wants less Les, less.

Some Things I'd Rather Not Know
(A Rant)

The modern mind must know everything,
Must reduce all sensual stimuli
To facts that look, and feel, and have the ring
Of steel – not feet of mealy clay.

It never seems to darken thought,
That our "facts" are always changing;
That the thing we swore upon last week is naught
In light of this week's rearranging.

A blooming nihilist I am not –
I know there are some verities,
But I'm so tired of being told that what
Was new last year, are this year's new antiquities.

Perfect Imperfection   Astigmatism

So if you'll pardon me, I think that I
Shall loosely hold to facts propounded –
Shall instead employ childhood's ample eye
And live my life, by wonders, full-astounded.

A cloud I'll call a blanket in the sky –
A thunderbolt, God's arrows –
Snowflakes, as they swirl and catch my eye,
I'll call God's snowy winter sparrows.

I'll read, and dream of lands, and wonder if
The land I see is like another that I long for –
A thought the factsters call naïf –
A land the factsters have no name for.

So forests deep I'll fill with fairies –
Oceans fill with mermaids.
Stars will sing, and earth will parry.
So will my labors – not laborious – be repaid.

Some things I'd rather not know;
To know destroys their mystery.
Besides, to "know," and find you did not know,
Is at worst, a fool's mastery.

The things I know, about clouds and thunder;
About forests, snow, and wintry sparrows;
About places deep and cool down under;
About oceans wide and rivers narrow,

Would make a modern factster groan;
Would put me in a class of fools,
Too simple to be counted on –
An idiot who froths and drools.

So, to please, I honor all their laws –
Especially the one on gravity –
But I'll not submit to all their saws
That change and change with tiresome regularity.

Pity not, my world is a stable one –
Predictably irregular.
Its irregularities are what I'm counting on;
And that its truths are singular.

The Mystery of Luminosity

My first remembered encounter with the moon occurred on a warm summer evening as our family was returning home from a church service and I saw the moon rising like a great orange-red ball beyond a fence and across a field. I asked my father, who was carrying me, to get it for me. Of course that was a request beyond even the powers of a loving and generous father, which he was. But in other ways, until his life ended at age 87, he continued "to give the moon" to his family and friends – to me. I sometimes wonder if he might also have given away his middle name at some point early in his life. For some reason he didn't have one.

This section of poems is dedicate to the memory of my Father, Glenn Rapp

Perfect Imperfection   The Mystery of Luminosity

Luna

That brilliant orb,
From which our globe
Was flung --
Too bright for us to look upon --
Another globe has spun,
Which, made in its own image,
And reflecting its own light,
Reveals its glorious visage
To our fragile, awestruck sight.

If you have seen the moon . . .
You have seen its sun.

Faithful Luna

Did you see her lying on her back:
A slender golden maiden dressed in black?
She seemed to be at rest tonight -
The golden bearer of the light
Was on a holiday - and what a sight
She made, a lovely maiden, slight
Of girth but elegantly long. One might
Be lured to fly up to her height
And try to take a tiny little mite
Of the gold she seems to hold by right.
Ah but there is neither will nor might
That can catch and hold her light.
And even she at end of night
Relinquishes its radiance bright,
Sending back in faithful flight
All her glory to the Giver of her light.

Our Luna-Friend

Luna is playing among the clouds tonight,
Her joy is to slowly fade from sight
And make us think she'll spend the night
Roaming the sky in secret flight.

But soon again we'll see her go
Through wispy clouds that gently flow
Across her face; a misty show
Of Luna's lovely golden glow.

Luna on a Cold, Cold, Night

What brings you out tonight, silver orb?
You shine so brightly in the eastern sky.
There must be some special reason why
This winter cold you willingly absorb.

You must be driven by a need to go
To heights where you can see Sol's golden head,
So braving cold, you leave the comfort of your bed
To coldly bask in friend-love's golden glow.

Come! Enjoy the Moon!

Sunday evening's ending soon,
'Neath a golden summer moon.
Let us grab our harps and tune
Them to the songs of loons.
Then we'll sing a soft cocoon,
Shaped by our own elven tune,
In which we'll dance until, too soon,
The day will come, and fade the moon.

A Joy Worth Waking For

Luna is a joy intended for sharing,
And she knows it.
Her habits are calculated,
Designed to turn the eye.

She comes, in every shape and shade,
To catch our eye,
And waits to hear us cry,
"Oh, see the beauty in the sky!"

How many of her risings
Have I seen in all these years?
And has she ever failed to awe,
To make me wish to share her glories?

The first, that I recall, came
On a balmy night in Illinois
When, in my father's arms, I spied
Her blood-red rising in the east.

She hovered low,
Beyond a fence, across a field;
In a child's mind,
Easily within a father's reach.

We shared a wish that night,
My dad and I,
I wished to hold the pretty moon,
He wished to make it so.

Last night she hovered low again
Hanging in the eastern sky,
Pale Gold this time, not red,
In a cold Wisconsin sky.

How I wished to capture her,
To share her beauty,
Point her out,
Make another see.

An now today you write to me,
And tell of Luna's soft presence
In your room last night,
A joy, to you, worth waking for.

Luna is a joy intended for sharing,
And she knows it.
Her habits are calculated,
Designed to turn the eye.

Naked Reflection

Remnants of a cold had forced me from my bed,
Sent me seeking some relief, some remedy,
And thus it was that I was led
Into the presence of her Golden Majesty.

Rising, naked, just above the eastern building tops,
Luna framed her glory in the half-circle of a window pane.
Resting where old Sol, her lover, often stops,
She caught him looking back,
        and gloried for a while within his flame.

And I, for just a moment, stood in dual light
Of Sun and Moon, and naked, let it shine on me,
And wondered if some distant star or planet might
Depend, for light, upon my willingness to naked be.

A postlude

And I, the Son, if naked, lifted up I be,
Will draw all men unto the light of me,
So, in my naked flesh, themselves they'll see;
Their sin and shame revealed,
and hanging naked on a tree.

Luna and Sol

Did you see Luna in the sky last night?
Sometime before mid-afternoon she took her flight;
At first, as dimly in the east, she caught Sol's light,
And then, as the day wore on, she grew more bright.

Luna's loveliness can only shine on us
As she reflects her lover's light, and thus
By bending Sol's bright beams she thrusts
Her image forth, increased a thousand lux.

Old Sol must have a pride of waiting lovers
Whom his regal brightness nightly covers;
In the stillness of a million nights he hovers
In reflected glory, first o're one, and then another.

And thus are born a million golden nights.

Eclipsed

I have felt, I think, what Luna felt
Tonight, when our earth intruded
Itself between her
And her lover's light.

She should have worn a golden pelt,
Instead of shivering in the dark, excluded;
Waiting for her love to stir
And warm her with his glory bright.

There have been times when I have felt
The chill of standing quite denuded,
Waiting for some "earth" to move
And free me from the chilling grip of night.

The Mystery of Luminosity

There is a dark side to Luna
That I never see.
That glorious, golden face she turns to me
Is only half the truth
Of who she is.
I wonder, could it be
That Sol is in the dark like me,
That he can only know and see
What Luna lets him see?

I'm more inclined to think that he
Is full aware,
And, that she,
In ignorance, imagines
She can live, in secrecy,
A life, half light, half dark.

But why would Sol, so generously
Display his glory on the face,
Of one who hides herself deceptively?
It just may be that he,
Who shines so powerfully,
Cannot but show his glory,
And that, reflected it must be,
On the face (or aft)
Of all materiality.

Making Mud Into Moonlight

Lovely Luna was high in the Southwest sky
   again tonight, for just a little while,
   before the clouds rolled in.
She is much nearer the bright star (Jupiter?)
   than she was the last time I saw her.
I suppose her main gift to us
   is the counter-gravitational pull she provides
   to help keep our earth in line,
   saving it from drifting too near the sun.
But for me that service pales
   compared to the beauty she adds to the night sky.
She is undoubtedly mere mud, as we are,
   but when Sol's light shines on her
   she becomes a golden glory.

An Invitation to Dance: Declined

We've just had twelve hours
Under Luna's changing light.
Last night she "rose" low in the east,
Full and golden.

Perfect Imperfection   The Mystery of Luminosity

As I walked among the trees
I saw her dance and play within their branches,
Outlining their dark forms,
Giving life to them,
Accentuating their jet blackness;
Deepest dark and golden light
Joining hands
To dance the night away,
Inviting me to stay and dance with them.
I paused to look -
Enjoyed -
But hurried on my way.
This morning she is shining, pale and high.
Driven from her eastern place among the trees,
By mighty Sol,
She fled into the western sky,
Alone.
Her black partner gone,
Banished at bright Sol's command,
Luna grows more pale,
A silver memory only,
Of the warm and golden presence
That, last night,
Invited me to dance.

An Eye Opener

For years we've argued about the meaning
    of the circle of stones on Salisbury Plain.
Did they, or didn't they
      intend them to aim at the stars,
      or cradle a sunrise,
      or prophesy a day of darkness?

But does it really matter
> what *they* intended if all *you* want
> is to stand and watch the precision of the sun,
> rising between two monstrous pillars?

I could not escape these thoughts this morning
> as I drove, on a "well-planned highway,"
> into a glorious sunrise.

Did that engineer err
> when he aimed that highway
> into a December sunrise,
> endangering the lives of hundreds of travelers?

Or was he some subversive sun worshipper,
> using his state salary and position
> to advance his secret faith?
>> (A study needs to be done
>> to see how many of his highways
>> point to the rising sun.)

It really doesn't matter (to me) why he did it.
I was grateful for the view –
> a great orange globe that rose and set,
> and rose and set,
> as I traveled up and down the hills.

They warn us that looking at the sun will result in blindness.
I felt, this morning, that it had the opposite effect.

Sol Rising

Sol, I saw you, glowing red,
> as you rose above the trees.

Perfect Imperfection   The Mystery of Luminosity

Beneath your gaze a dealer's lot
   contained a hundred cars,
   made by ambivalent men
   who paint their wares
   to catch your rays
   and raise the praise
   of their designs,
   but fight,
   with wax and shades,
   your withering fire
   that burns and fades
   their lovely "skins"
   and cracks their rubber tires.

What are you, Sol?
Our father? Brother? Cousin?
Are we flesh of your flesh,
   bone of your bone?
Did our Maker, in some distant day
   take a rib from you
   and shape from it
   our earth,
   or do we both derive our life
   from some other
   ancient cosmic mother?

You wear your fire upon your face,
   we carry ours within our gut,
   but wonder if, in distant days,
   we did not also burn as you,
   and over countless centuries,
   our heat and passion lose.

Concentrated Light

Poems use a number of means to capture our attention, pulling us out of our usual prosaic existence and forcing us to view the world in some new and unexpected way. Often they become prisms, combining strands of light to focus, laser-like, on things the poet wants to show us.

This section of poems is dedicated to the memory of my mother, whose formal education did not reach the 8th grade, but who nonetheless modeled for her children a life of learning and achievement, earning a high school diploma late in life after producing scores of poems that are now the treasure of her children and grandchildren. And along the way she introduced her children to story after story with her evening reading sessions. In a pre-television era the family was treated almost daily to readings, children lounging around the room and dad snoozing in his chair, responding with an "Uh huh" each time he was asked, "Glenn, are you listening?". Thus we were introduced to many volumes of good literature, one chapter at a time.

To the memory of my mother, Rena Faye (Kennerly) Rapp.

Perfect Imperfection Concentrated Light

Perfect Imperfection

Lord, I often wished that I could sing a song to you
Not sung before;
With thoughts that tell my heart's desire to do
Your will – to open up its door
Releasing words whose syllables no mind has ever bent
In rhyme, or rhythm, order, or intent,
To praise our God Omnipotent.

It would not be a polished thing; the rules of poetry
I've never learned.
It would be a gift of simple peasant artistry –
Hand made – not finely turned;
No anthems, no soaring hymns – A row of shells
Upon a string;
But it would say   uniquely say – as never said so well,
The thing – the wondrous thing –
My swelling heart would sing if it could tell.

But I am torn – two thoughts have been impressed
Upon my mind.
One says that nothing new has ever been expressed;
No new thing, of any kind
Has, ever since the sun was set, been thought or done,
Or ever could.
The other says that God is ever making new; that not one
Mite or chip of wood
Is like another He has made or hued.

A child I heard, once, sing a new song, though to sing it new
Was not the child's intent.
To sing a song that filled his heart was all he thought to do;
To sing – and be content.
His mind the words and meanings changed; the melodies confused.

As through his lips they came,
We, standing by, with knowledge of the true, were amused;
We smiled – a child's game!
But to the heart of God it rose, a song anew.

So I've decided, Lord, I'll sing my song to you, of peasant artistry,
A row of shells, poor strung.
It may well be – as the wisest said – in all of human history
No new thing was ever done;
That every thought and word does naught
But give to you, upon inspection,
Your own thoughts back.
But may you hear your child's fumbling words and missed inflection –
Smile – forgive his lack,
And hear a new song, sung in perfect imperfection.

Not My Words, But Thine

Lord, on borrowed legs I come,
My breath, your breath, in-breathed.
With thoughts I did not know to think,
With words my lips can only feebly form,
A prayer, they pray.
Words, not my own, but of your making,
Shape the things I say.
It is a grace that you would call me to yourself
Through words I pray by inspiration;
Words appearing to be mine
Are yours, lent to this speechless mind;
A gracious verbal incarnation.

Concentrated Light

A poem is the condensation
        of a thought,
A crafted incarnation,
        often dearly bought,
Of a song or sorrow,
Taking wide
        and making narrow
Some dear moment,
Some dear memory,
Some illumination,
Shaping it,
        in focused concentration,
Into a jewel,
        shining, through it's facets,
Truth too wide to be explained
        in ordinary speech.

Heart Work

Sometimes the heart just aches
Because it is a thinking, feeling thing.
Ever searching for the word that makes
The meaning of its "lyrics" ring,
It tries them all, and then it takes
The best, and pounding, makes the anvil sing
Until the song it shapes
Reflects the image of its inner scenes.

The Best Use of The Best Words

Tell me, then, why words gain
Power when they're rearranged
And made to speak with all the force
The writer's mind commands.

It doesn't seem they need to rhyme,
Or that they have to be in certain orders;
They can be quite ordinary words
And still command attention.

"The best use of the best words,"
My teacher once told me,
"Is the measure of a poem," so the greater the
Mind, the greater the product will be.

"The best use of the best words" . . .
That would make each word of God a poem,
The word that spoke the universe to be,
Is heaven's grandest poetry.

The word that sent the Word to us,
Enfolded in human flesh, the Word itself
That came to live and die
Is poetry; life saving, soul saving poetry.

The Word that, hidden in my heart,
Shines forth upon my way,
To keep my feet from stumbling,
And leads me in His way, is poetry.

And when I hear Him say,
"Well done! Come in."
I'll know my ears have heard the poem,
For which they've waited longingly.

The name that God will someday speak to me,
Naming all the things in me He sees –
Things His power has caused to come to be –
Will be, to me, a word of glorious poetry.

Introspection

What drives a poet to write more?
Perhaps it is that last verse,
The one just ushered through the door
Unwashed, unfed, ill clad, or worse.

There is always hope that his next "child"
Will bear the marks of noble, ancient ancestry;
Will resemble some forgotten kinfolk mild
And not the face reflected in his recent poetry.

What drives a poet to write another verse?
The fear that his last might be remembered -
What a desperate curse -
To go to poet's heaven thus encumbered.

What drives a poet to produce more words?
"Last words," he knows, often are the measure
By which time, the judge, accords
"Thumbs up" or "thumbs down" at the mob's pleasure.

Truth Tellers

God is not a myth,
But myth may be
The only means
By which we come
To know Him.

In pristine Eden
God was seen
Face to face
And known
Heart to heart.

But ever since
We know Him only
Through the stories
Told of Him –
Man-made stories.

Except for one brief
Glorious moment,
When God incarnate said,
"If you have seen Me,
You have seen the Father,"

Holy men of old,
Flawed earthen vessels,
Have crafted stories,
Under inspiration,
That tell of Him.

And still today
Flawed men and women –
Inspired and set apart –
Craft their art
To tell of Him,

Some to great acclaim,
Some in simple testimony,
All attempts to frame
In human frailty
The image or their Maker.

All stories that
Fail to tell of Him,
At best, are worthless;
At worst they are
Demonic lies.

God is not a myth
But myth may be
The only earthly means
By which we come
To know Him.

On Sources of Inspiration

Where do the words and thoughts come from
That seed my brain? Are they the sum
Of all my years . . . of all my learning?
What fires my heart - sets my brain to burning?

I have no answers, only questions;
Some things come easily, but I must wrest some
From the deep recesses of my thought,
And those take time - are dearly bought.

Others come bounding forth
Clamoring for all their worth,
Leaping, pre-made, to their place in line,
Filled with meaning, grace, and rhyme.

But either way, when long they've lain,
I cannot recognize their face again;
"No sons of mine are these", I say,
Another, better far than I, some Workman, fey,
      has come, and left them on my tablet lay.

The Meaning of Silence

The apparent emptiness of Silence
Is a problem words cannot resolve,
Because Silence is not always absence;
Often it is filled, as roiling thoughts devolve.

So I never know if Silence is meant to speak to me,
Of if it is the product of distraction;
If it is showing, without words, things I aught to see,
Of if I may, in safety, consider it a thoughtless action.

But would I choose a world with no verbal voids?
Do I assume that such a world would make me see
More clearly, things I need to do – things I should avoid?
Or is Silence just another part of the language that we speak?

Praise

Lewis says that we delight to praise what we enjoy -
To compliment alone is not our goal, but to employ
Our praise as a tangible element of that alloy
We seek to forge; the object is the joy.

To see a scene of sharable worth,
Or hear some tale of share-worthy mirth,
And have no one with which to share is worse
Than half a joy; it is a joy still-birthed.

But if we could find a way to "get it out";
To tell the one whose praise it's all about,
How beautiful they are, and leave no doubt,
Then would our delight be fully carried out.

And the higher the object of our praise
The greater our heart's desire to raise
A paean suitable to say, in flawless ways,
The joy we see that makes us praise.

The object is the joy; knowing that our groping word
Of praise encompasses to gird
That beauty that we see,
Naming not alone, but helping it to be.

Wonderful Memories

I've been reading poems
    written when my heart was full,
And with the reading comes
    a thousand thoughts to mull.

A thousand reasons merged,
        those poems to inspire,
And now a thousand memories urge
        me warm myself at their bright fire.

The Poet's Sword

There are three things
   that every poet needs;
     three loves, three wings,
       three swift and sturdy steeds.
     To make his poems sing
   he cannot fail to heed
these three imaginings.

He must love words;
   their sound and beat and meaning.
     He must embrace the teeming world;
       Its many sights and smells and feelings.
     But more than all he needs Woman
   to inspire his deepest, clearest seeing;
Isha, the poet's sharpest sword!

A Resolution From A Very Wordy Man

Since words prove impotent to bear my thought,
Why do I ramble on and on?
I'll speak a few, with deepest meaning fraught,
And, with a smile, be gone.

I'll speak of faith, and hope, and love,
All things, when spoke without alloy,
That lift our thoughts to things above;
And thus, I'll always speak with joy.

What is a poem?

A poem can be a sermon,
    flatly telling it "like it is."
A poem can be a lecture,
    researched, outlined and delivered.
But the best poem is an invitation to ponder;
An inspiration, a breath, an inhalation,
    of truth not yet fully unveiled.

As You Have Said, Let It Be Unto Me

Part 1

No one loves a dog who ties it to a tree,
Makes it heel, or sit, or fetch,
Scolds it when it barks, or drapes it in a shawl.

Dogs are made to run and wander free,
To dig and sniff; to hunt and chase and catch;
To snarl and growl; to bully and to brawl.

Oh true, some may love their Spot,
But scold him when he's being dog;
Their love is for a "dog" that's not.

True love for dog is only got
By letting dog be truly dog;
Insisting that it not be what it's not.

Part 2

Mary, did you ever rue your words,
"Lord, I am your servant;
As you have said, let it be it unto me."?

The baby, born, was bound to you with fleshly cords.
You could have claimed it as *your* infant;
Used your mother-love to shape, direct, its destiny.

But you declared and proved yourself, to be a servant –
Of your God, and of the Gift he birthed in you –
You let the Gift teach *you* the role that you should play:

To incarnate the Son of God in form of human infant,
But resist the human urge to make Him bow to *you*.
Instead, you watched Him choose the awful role He came to play.

Part 3

Man, *inspired* by God, became a breathing *kind*,
Inspiring, expiring . . . a fleeting gift, for sure,
 "My breath will not always abide in man, henceforth."

Incarnation and inspiration are two of a kind.
Through *incarnation* Mary's Word was born in her;
Through *inspiration* Isaiah's Word went forth.

God, through *inspiration,* wants to breathe His truth in all,
Truth become incarnate . . . for the common good.
Inspired Truth – Expired Truth, delivered faithfully . . .

By *evangels*, refusing, anything not dog, a dog to call;
Naming what *is*, what it truly *is*, for the common good!
Insisting, Lord, as you have said, let it be unto me.

On Reviewing My Poetry

I've been sorting through my thoughts -
The many, many poems that I've wrought -
And thinking that the thing I most had ought,
Was to use the education that my parents bought.

But no use crying over milk that's spilt,
I'm in this thing up to the hilt;
It is the house of poetry that Jimmy built,
A patchwork mess, a crazy quilt.

But I can no more throw the stuff away
Than end this evening wishing not another day.
This is bone of my bone, so what can I say,
I must redeem my words that have gone astray.

And many there are that are wayward words,
Not saying at all what my heart averred.
When I penned them, angelic expressions I heard;
Whence comes, now, this cacophonous herd?

Perfect Imperfection   Concentrated Light

Braying donkeys and grabbling geese,
Fumbling words that could never release
The vision by which the muses I'd please . . .
I'm thinking, alas, the muses came only to tease.

But I'll work gamely on – it is what "poets" do –
To correct my errors, with a choice word or two,
Knowing the things I change or write new,
Will cry out again to be changed . . . the next time through.

What Mean These Stones?

If we are lucky – and observant – we will see, when looking back over our lives, many "memorial stones"; people, places, events, thoughts, occasions. They are the things of which our lives were constructed and, in the end will be the memories that enrich our final, thoughtful days.

> Memory –
>   all that's left of everything.

This section of poems is dedicated to the memory of two teachers whose influence has lingered and blessed my life.

Ruby Matthews was my sixth grade teacher. A beautiful, round-faced, kind-spoken woman with snow white hair. It was her reading to us, a chapter a day, of wonderful books that I credit, in part, with my early interest in good books.

Winifred Rhodes, my sophomore English teacher, by defining poetry as, "The best use of the best words," gave me hope, late in my life, that I could perhaps shape words deserving of the name of "poetry".

Perfect Imperfection   What Mean These Stones?

In Memoriam

A set of knives, a little tin box,
A plumb bob, or an old shirt;
The things we save that locks,
In time, those now gone, and girts,
With love, their memory.

This poem was inspired by a conversation
with Cheryl (Seidel) Brandt and commemorates
things saved in memory of Arlen and Sylvia Seidel
and Glenn and Rena Faye Rapp

Honor

I've been thinking about honor lately;
It's not something you seek
But something you give.

Honors sought are innately
Inferior and often beset
With burdens corrosive.

But honors bestowed
Are like "bread on the water",
Returning to bless the giver.

A Mother's Day Poem for My Wife

Because you were there
I saw you
Because you were pretty
I liked what I saw
Because you were gentle
You drew me to you
Because you were honest and good
I began to love you
Because you believed in me
I dared to hope
Because you encouraged me
I asked for your love
Because you loved me
I asked for your hand
Because you gave it
I'm one happy man!

What We Know About Friendship

Friendship
   is knowing you belong,
knowing it is right for you
   to be there,
knowing you are
   the possession of.

Friendship
   is knowing you possess,
knowing that possessing
   is not controlling,
knowing that possessing
   is caring for.

Friendship
   is knowing how to give,
knowing what and
   when to give,
knowing the value
   of what you give.

Friendship
   is knowing how to take,
knowing what
   is yours to take,
knowing what
   must not be taken.

Friendship
   is knowing about forever,
knowing the
   eternal now,
knowing that
   the future can't be had.

The Wonder of A Photograph
*(A poem to friend accompanied
by a photograph of flowers the friend
had previously give us.)*

The wonder of a photograph
Is that it takes us back in time
Along a winding, mystic path,
To mem'ry's balmy clime.

It takes us to a magic hour;
To a place our hearts have been;
To a place where friendship's bower
Is alive with friendship's scents.

It reminds us, in its gentle way,
Of a thoughtfulness that came
From a friend who'd been away,
But remembered, just the same.

And it serves to let us
Show her, on her very special day,
How the beauty that she sent us
Blooms again to bless *her*,
　　in a pictographic way.

Have a very happy birthday, Friend!

An Ode To Three Wonderful Boys
(Aaron James, Isaac Maxwell, Jacob David)

I've said that I would
Make a list of words,
Designed, as best I could,
To trumpet to the world
The kind of "sons"
That I've "inherited" –
In actual fact, grandsons,
I've somehow merited.

AARON JAMES, the oldest,
STRONG, when faced with tests,
PROTECTOR of the family's nest,

A MEDIATOR when a sibling quarrel fest's.
At LOVING others, he's the best,
THOUGHTFUL of the needs of all the rest,
SENSITIVE, his heart . . . his hands. He invests
His time to be an ARTIST .

ISAAC MAXWELL, second son,
Is INWARD, finding things that can be done
In quiet ways. WITTY, always loving fun;
"Laughter" is the meaning given to this son.
LOVING others, FAITHFUL as the morning sun,
SENSITIVE and GRATEFUL is this one;
GENTLE . . . THOUGHTFUL, is this second son.

JACOB DAVID, the last and the first,
OUTWARD, ACTIVE, moving with a burst
Of energy. INTELLECTUAL, with a thirst
For knowledge of the best and worst.
CURIOUS about all things, he goes, headfirst.
LOVING and GREGARIOUS, from last to first.

What Mean These Stones
(A Small Comfort to Mound-makers)

Our spiritual fathers strewed their world with piles of stones,
Reminders of numinous encounters with their God,
Attempts to build within their world some sacred zones
Where generations after them would worship as their fathers had.

I wonder what my hapless successors will choose to make
Of the memorial mess with which I've strewn my way;
Mute mounds commemorate false starts and things half-baked.
Gathering dust on floor and desk, they wait on judgment day.

Those who leave no mounds are the envy of all mound-makers;
Their lives, uncluttered, indict our cluttered-ness.
But God will be the judge; sorting through our piles, our Maker
May find evidence of some feeble, fumbling God-ward-ness.

A "Song" for Bud & Pat
(For their 50th Anniversary)

Love and marriage are good things,
Made in heaven; sealed on earth with rings;
Ever growing, ever encircling bands,
Forged to be worn on ever inclusive, ever receptive hands.

True bands of marriage aren't made of gold
But of purer stuff, meant to hold
Together a love that, by skeptics we're told,
Will diminish with time; that is sure to grow cold.

But the special character of a true wedding band
Is that it grows stronger as it is stretched and expands
To include more and more lives in its firm embrace;
As it seeks, a larger, more inclusive, circle to trace.

The bands that encircled your wedding day
Felt cozily small and seemed to say,
"Our world is our world . . . let all stay away;
We two are enough, leave us alone to love and play!"

But God knew what a band that small would do,
How it would strangle your love and draw you into
A spiral of selfishness with shrinking walls,
Ending the mission to which true love calls.

Perfect Imperfection What Mean These Stones?

So slowly He let you come to see
What a true wedding band was meant to be;
How it never, in truth, was meant to be small;
How it ever seeks to encompass all.

So today, after fifty good years
Of mixing heart-filling laughter with unwanted tears,
We stand encircled in a marvelous band;
In the circle you've made by the reach of your hands.

A Valentine Poem

Daughter dear, you live your days,
With Paradise near, and flowery leis
That rival the ancient mythic ways
When Eden's golden age held sway.
So a rose such as this,
May evoke no bliss,
But it speaks great volumes to me,
For I think of a Miss
We delighted to kiss
When she was a "tea-rose" of three.
And now that you've grown --
Come into your own --
This rose more accurately shows
The beauties, mature,
That grow and endure –
You're a prize, as everyone knows.

A Valentine's Day Poem

Valentines are for kids and girls, I know.
But if that's the case then how's a Dad to show
The things about his son that make him proudly glow;
Things he'd like the whole wide world to know?

No, Valentines must be for everyone;
For pets, and friends . . . especially sons,
And this one I am counting on
To tell you what you've gone and done.

You've given joy to Mom and me
In blessings, multiplied by three –
Three boys that we can weekly see,
And hold, and love abundantly.

But more than that, I want to say
How much *you* bless us every day,
By things you are, and do, and say;
A son who makes us proud, a hundred ways.

A Valentine's Day Prayer

Father, thank you for a daughter dear,
Whose fortunes, hopes, and joys are near
To Your heart, so we need never fear,
But commit her to Your hand to steer.

Bless her with Your abundant love,
And may she ever look to You, above all other friends,
And always seek the counsel of Your Word, and then
Obey in all You tell her of.

May she never doubt her mother's love, nor mine.
May she always know our loves entwine
Her interest. But may she always, ever find
Her greatest joy in Your designs.

For A Nurse-Friend Watching Her Father Die

This is a journey of which you'll not miss a step.

You've been a guide for other's itinerary
And yet
Your knowledge of the trail was fragmentary -

Small pieces of learning you've gained;
Short visits in the halls of pain,
Brief talks with the dying - then home again,
Leaving the walking to the lame.

But now, dear Heart, the trail is yours, each step.

No longer a guide - a traveler now you are,
And yet
Your knowledge of the trail will carry you far.

Miss no scenes as you travel along.
Cherish each sigh, each moan, each song.
Hold each moment - try not to prolong;
Accept God's will with faith that is strong.

This is a journey your Father has set

To make you a blessing for others who yearn
To get
From your words what travel alone can learn.

The Matriculation of A Young Lady

Since "graduation" is a strange way
To describe the special kind of day
That, recently, you've reached, I may
Choose to describe it in another, clearer way.

Of course you reached that day in increments;
Gradually achieving expertise that compliments
The vast array of facts and arguments
You carry, now, about with confidence.

So in a broad and cosmic sense, I guess,
That day of "graduation" is no more nor less
Than an increment, a marker of progress,
Along the path to life's success.

But it seems that something's changed now;
Something new is born that will endow
Your nascent gifts and finally allow
A fuller view of "really you" to show.

Would "Grand Opening" or "Under New Management" do?
Perhaps "New Version" would better describe you.
Or even "De-bugged, Enhanced, Enlarged, and Made New";
Something, at least, to show your breakthrough.

But those are so crass for one of your class,
So I'll suggest, instead, that we say that a lass
Of dear charm has matriculated; that now, at long last,
She is a woman of promise – always a promise – but now recast.

In Memory of Sylvia – A Dear Friend
(Died May 27, 2008)

Some gifts come early and linger long,
Renewing, daily, all their benefice;
By being, blessing, time and time again.

Others, barely sensed before they're gone,
Impressions only, a breath upon our face,
Leave, nonetheless, a blessing deep within.

To her family, Sylvia's blessing lingered long,
To me it seemed a breath upon my face,
In all, she left a lasting memory,
       that comes to fill our hearts,
              time . . . and time again.

Father of fathers
*(Written for the anniversary of the death
of a Godly father.)*

I thank you, Father God, on this special day,
For a father, the blessing of whom –
The value of whom – no one can weigh.
Not because I lost him so soon;

Not because I loved him so dearly;
Not because he loved me so well.
All true, but more, through him, you clearly
Displayed Yourself – used him to tell

What "Heavenly Father" should mean to me;
Used him as an earthly reflection
So, in him, I could see
An image, though dim, of Your Perfection.

Perfect Imperfection   What Mean These Stones?

He was not perfect,
Nor would make such a claim,
But even his defects,
Admitted . . . repented, became

Echoes, examples, sculptures, in mirrored relief,
Of fatherhood, by the Father recurved,
Displaying, in frailty, the grand motif
Of the Father in Heaven he served.

Saying, "See the good that is in me?
The Father is infinitely higher.
See what I am not, though I wish to be?
That is the Father's image, to which I aspire."

Thank you, Father of Love,
For revealing yourself afresh.
In father you showed me something of
Yourself, sending a picture of You in the flesh.

For his faithfulness, goodness, tenderness, and fairness, I thank you!
For his humor, patience, faith, and wisdom, I thank you!
For his provision, steadfastness, courage, and strength, I thank you!
For the reflection he gave me of You, Father God, I thank you!

Thank you, Ruth and Arlene!

Over the weeks we've been blessed;
Been fed and feted, given the best
Of your food, and allowed to rest
In the comfort of your cozy nest.

In your home we've met to love and to share,
To laugh, and to learn, and to join in prayer.
Sister to sister we've divided our cares,
By sharing the burdens of each who is there.

And sister to sister our joys we've increased;
By adding Love's alloy we've weekly released
The aroma of friendship, of comfort and peace,
And thus, in our Friend-love, our cares are eased.

Thank you, dear friends for having us here.
May God bless you by making it clear
To your hearts that His Spirit is near,
At Christmas, of course, but all through the year.

(A poem written, at the request of my wife, to accompany a gift given to two friends for hosting a women's weekly prayer and share time.)

A Cup of Warm II

Even when we're miles apart,
our cups are raised in friendship,
and when their nectar touches lip,
it makes, of two, or more, one heart.

So grab a cup of warm, dear friends,
and we will feel the friendship
through every thought-filled sip we sip
and every word we send and get.

To Allison
(A birthday Poem)

Oh, the memories that come,
When thinking of that one
Precious answer to our orison;
An infant joy, a rising sun,
A promise - and a gift - that one
Could hold and cherish long;
Our dear, enfolded Allison.

Oh, the joy of watching, from
A distance, the maturing sun,
Sitting higher as each year was done;
Passing over, passing on,
Pouring warmth and brightness down;
Our sunny, funny Allison.

Oh, the hope - the prayer - dear Allison,
That your life be filled with "fun";
But even more, be filled with SON,
Be made aware of what God's done -
He put His name in Alli-SON;
Our precious, everlasting Allison

A Birthday Blessing
(To a friend on his 70th birthday)

This comes to wish you more than happiness,
Though happiness we wish, without alloy,
Nay, more than pleasure, based on that or this,
We wish you baseless, senseless, soul-deep joy!

Not based on things this world calls real,
Not sensible to hand or eye or ear,
Yea, something that the heart alone can feel,
A joy that tells you, "God is near."

The "Story" of Dan
(In memory of a friend who died of Parkinson's disease)

Ah, Dan!
Your book is written, the pen laid by.
We turn its pages, and read and sigh,
Seeing connections our minds had passed by;
Seeing the man God knew, and why
He wrote the Book of Dan.

Oh Dan!
For a decade or so, I've been reading your book.
To know the whole story I'd need to look
To others who know much better the paths that you took;
The things you've done; the things forsook,
That make up your story – the Story of Dan.

And Dan,
I want you to know – I've told you before –
That the story I read inspires me far more
Than stories of fame, fortune, or wealth stored;
Yours is a story of earth moved and pain ignored
By the will of a wonderful, faithful man.

Yes Dan,
The pages I've read are at the end of your book,
Telling of sickness, and pain, and the effort it took –
But you willed to be useful and faithfully looked
For ways to bless others, and never forsook
The path of a God-fearing man.

So Dan,
Your book is written – its message is plain,
It shows that life's sunshine may turn to rain;
But true strength will win over suffering and pain.
Stumbling, falling, it rises, again and again,
Revealing the strength of a God-fearing man.

A Wish For Joy
(To My Wife)

This message is, my dear,
A wish for you that flows,
A stream of never ending joy;
A joy that goes beyond beyond;
A joy that won't, in time, abscond;
In short, a joy without alloy,
That grows and grows and grows
 With every passing year.

A Pastor

A Pastor is a Shepherd,
      Feeding, guiding, healing sheep.
A Pastor is a Watchman,
      Driving Satan's "shepherds" from the keep.
A Pastor is a Teacher,

    Sowing thoughts whose roots go deep.
A Pastor is a Brother,
    Who can weep with those who weep.
But more than all of these,
    Unlike those who honor seek,
A Pastor is a Servant,
    Taking towels, and washing feet.

The Renaming of Jacob

Once I heard discussion
Of how I came to be named,
Almost becoming, David William
Instead of James.

Thus I could have been,
"Beloved Protector,"
Rather than
"The heel-puller, beloved."

I must presume my parents
Knew a James who, in their opinion
Was no heel-puller, and a David
Who was truly beloved.

Unless, of course, they saw in me
Traits of character
That the world
Needed warning of.

Biblical Jacob came from the womb
With his hand around the heel
Of his just born sibling, Esau,
Evoking delight in those who named him.

But they were less than pleased
When he self-servingly withheld the stew
From famished Esau, saying, "I'll let go
When you sell to me your blessing."

Were his parents prophets
Who clearly saw his course at birth,
Or did they set his course for life
By the name they gave him?

The angel felt his stubborn grip,
Wrestling through the night with him,
Heard him breathlessly insist,
"I'll not let go until you bless me."

God, who had another name for Jacob,
Used his heel-grasping tenacity
To make of him a new-named man,
Israel, a prince who prevailed with God.

Every one of us is named: at birth,
In kindergarten, on the playground,
At work, by friends and lovers,
And by those who have no love for us.

We can choose to be what others name us,
Or like Jacob, wrestle with our better angel,
Refusing to release our grip on him,
Until he blesses and re-names us.

On Loving (or not) The Wrinkles

Love that stops where the wrinkles begin
Is selfish, incomplete love,
Asking of the other
What neither the loved nor the lover can give.

Love that stops when the wrinkles begin
Cherishes only the moment,
Misses a lifetime of love,
And was never really a love at all.

Love that can't see past the wrinkles
Is a short-sighted love,
Missing the hidden perfections;
The beauties of heart, mind, and soul.

Love that doesn't love the wrinkles
Is a stingy love,
Giving itself only in part,
Or, more to the point, not at all.

Two Rocks

Two rocks tumbled slowly,
Carried by the glacial movement
Of the flowing mass
Of other stones
In which they swam,
Until they touched.
And then awoke the sense
That there was meaning
In the touch;

Perfect Imperfection   What Mean These Stones?

Meaning in the dance
That turned them,
Ever touching,
'Til no edge
Had been untouched.
Two rocks bore no resemblance
When they met,
Or if they did
It was by chance,
But at the end
The tumbling dance
Had made of them
A matched set -
A perfect pair.

The Prophet's Eye

The prophet's task is to *see* what others cannot, do not, or will not see, and then to *tell* what he or she has seen. The prophet lives precariously; in some eras, and in some parts of the present world, she plies her trade at risk of losing her life, as did Anna Stepanovna Politkovskaya, the Russian journalist who was assassinated in 2006 for her reporting on the abuses of power by the Russian government in Chechnya.

Being a "prophet" in the United States is not without risk either as the deaths of Martin Luther King, Jr., Malcolm X, and any number of civil rights activists testify.

For me to entitle this section "The Prophet's Eye" may seem, to some, presumptuous. To some degree it seems so to me. The poems included are not likely to inflame passions in the way those "prophets" mentioned above have done. But the poems do point to injustices and, to use a thoroughly outdated word, sins of our day.

Every "prophet" needs supporters. For two decades I have had the loyal support of Steven and Cheryl Brandt. They have not agreed with all that I have written but they have given me the freedom to speak without fear of losing their faithful friendship.

So, without in any way implying their endorsement of any particular idea expressed in these poems I dedicate this section to our good friends, Steven and Cheryl Brandt.

The Prophet's Eye

*Formerly in Israel, if a man went to enquire of God,
he would say, "Come, let us go to the seer," because
the prophet of today used to be called a seer. 1Samuel 9:9*

In ancient Sumer *seers* used to earn their way
By insightful observation – how sheep's entrails lay –
Then advising, for a *seer's* fee, the propitious day
To attack a foe, to take a bride, or when to harvest hay.

In early Israel, the process seemed to be the same;
One sought to find a *seer* of distinctive fame
Who, for a fee, would make the *seer*'s standard claim;
That he, or she, the patron's future could proclaim.

The years have hidden from us all the ways and means
Those ancient Hebrew *seers* used, the hidden "truth" to glean;
They "flipped a coin", sought yes or no, it sometimes seems –
Urim? *Thummim*? Black stone? White stone? – Choose between.

But then, as time went on, a different class of *seers* rose;
Austere men who dared to call the early *seers'* "game", a pose;
Only *prophets*, called and sent by God they said, could know
The hidden truths – and hidden sins – that time would otherwise
    disclose.

By *inspiration* - by the Spirit *breathing in* –
True prophets saw, as though around a hidden bend,
Not the future only, but more often present, secret sins;
Affairs men didn't want the prophets meddling in.

The Prophet's Eye

Since God himself could not be seen,
The wicked felt that nothing stood between
Their predatory ways, too oft unseen,
And the victims that their practices "picked clean."

But God is ever seeing, ever standing nigh,
Hearing, heeding, grieving every injured party's cry,
Revealing to His prophets every slight and every lie,
Hiding nothing from His prophet's faithful eye.

Someday, we're told, we'll no more need to hear
The prophet's voice; that everything will be made clear;
That all will have the eyes to see, and ears to hear,
And hearts that long to bring God's kingdom near.

But more than ever now, we need the prophet's eye,
Trained to see, and then reveal, the subtle hidden lie,
Standing firm for righteousness – not afraid to raise the cry,
"Repent! Unless we change, all that's good and true will die."

Too many "seer prophets", mere forecasters, strive to be,
Predicting when the world will end, or unforeseen catastrophe,
But what is needed desperately, are prophets, truly led to see
A sinful, broken world; who dare declare it so . . . prophetically.

A Work Deferred For Lack of Purity

I have spent this whole day forgetting something I knew,
Early in the morning, the Spirit was leading me to do.
I do not mean that I have forgotten it all day
And just now, at bedtime recall, what I heard Him say.
I've been actively forgetting, purposeful, knowing without doubt,
That I was refusing to do the thing He spoke about.

Part of what He'd have me do is attractive, easy to respond;
It fits with all my prejudices so I could gladly sound
An alarm against those sins – mostly sins of other men;
The pre-dawn hours I spent in thought outlining them.
But then the thought of my mind's sin – my own wicked heart
Smote me, and now I am not so eager – fearful, really am I – to start.

Why do I say I love the Truth but quail before its light?
Can I say, "I hate the Lie!" when, finding one in me, I refuse to fight
Its ensnaring encroachments, its Truth-killing blight?
Can you, oh God, use deceitful lips and hearts not right?
I fear to start because . . . where this will go full well I know,
And I must just as surely know that there my will will go.

I've been reading that the righteous fire of God is hottest
When we stand apart, when we draw back from the test,
But that those who run into its core find it cool,
Refreshing! And when they naked downward look, a pool
Of emptiness they see, and the ashes of the useless husks
They once thought worthy of esteem and trust.

Perfect Imperfection 　　　　　　　　The Prophet's Eye

A new day is here; I'd like to take up your work, Lord – now.
But now the bright fire is but a smoldering coal – how
Can I revive it? Is the mission still your heart and soul?
Or have you found another who will do it free and whole?
Or was it just a test to see if I loved Truth and You
Enough to kill the Lie in me and live the True.

Lord, I dare not say I've yielded all when still my heart is fearful.
Perfect love casts out all fear, granting peace that, cheerful,
Lays aside old loves, old hopes, old sins, old lies
Without a thought of loss – no moans, complaints or sighs –
And goes to do the thing you said – and does the task
As though it were his own best will, because his Father asked.

No Abraham am I – the only thing you asked today, I have not done –
He quickly rose, took in hand his son, his only son,
And climbed the mount with only hope to guide,
And there to God, his only God, he yielded up his hope and pride.
With hope then given, and only promise of a progeny,
He offered even that to God, the only God he could not see.

Truth

Truth cannot always show
That the words She speaks
Are verifiable fact.
For Truth is seldom meant to show
The things a mere fact-finder seeks.
Truth takes a different tack.

In doing so She is not being coy.
Facts, hard facts, must always *know*;
Must everything *explain*.

Truth, so often forged in faith - with no alloy -
Her certainties, things she cannot show -
Flashes forth, then disappears again.

So can she then be truly true
If facts cry out against her?
Are not facts the final judge?
Or shall the facts, by Truth, be judged anew;
Made to lay their "certainties" before Her,
Surrendering their subterfuge?

Thinking About Man's Use of Time

Man, who began to chunk off time in years --
Vessels large enough to hold the tears
His careless ways would generate -- fears
Now they will not hold enough of things that cheer,
And so, in nanoseconds, subdivides his years,
And finds, alas, the nanoseconds filled with lonely fears.

The Danger of "Knowing" The Truth

The man most in danger
Is the one who holds a strong opinion.
His positions have no range or
Flexibility, and turn only on the narrow pinion
Of his stale repeated repertoire.

The Scribes and Pharisees were such men
Who would rather keep a cherished lie
Than let a new idea in
For fear that it might force a new perspective
By shining light on all their "righteous" sin.

A Prayer For Peace

It would take a thousand, thousand years,
Immersed in countless bitter tears,
Surrounded and engulfed in fears,
With no hope that helps or cheers,
To requite the grief they've borne,
Of the bodies racked and torn,
By the shells, and hate's cruel storms,
Hopelessly and helplessly forlorn.
And even that would not repay
For a single anguished day,
Watching innocents who lay,
Bleeding precious life away.

God, who through eternity's long years,
Have beheld your own Son's tears;
Comforted his anguish-spoken fears -
Come now - draw this broken planet near.

Justice
(A Retrospective Look at Jury Duty)

What is justice?
Is it satisfied because an accused man
Is condemned and punished for a crime?
As though guilt could ever be known
 . . . for sure.

Is justice done
When twelve are convinced (or merely conned)
Beyond "reasonable doubt" that one who,
Moments before, was "innocent"
 . . . is no longer?

Is justice decided
By a contest of strategies that tells
Only that amount of truth necessary to "prove" a point
. . . beyond "reasonable doubt"?

Is it justice
When witnesses, sworn to tell the "whole truth",
Are led by lawyers, for and against, to reveal
. . . only selected "truth"?

Is justice justice at all
When those deciding innocence and guilt
Are muzzled, fed only the miserly "truth"
. . . of professional obscurantists?

Is justice honored
When judges sleep, and defenders slouch;
When jurors, forced to be prosecutors and defenders,
. . . are only half informed?

Is justice served
When the accused is thrown a meatless bone
Of defense, scarred by the teeth of all the paupers
. . . who've chewed it before?

Can it be called justice
That those "innocent until proven guilty"
Only go free by the unanimous vote
. . . of the ill-informed?

Ah, Justice! How you must weep!

Living In The Shadow of a Shadow

How long did Peter's shadow hold its power?
Was it a life-long gift or given only for that hour?
The latter, I imagine, though we aren't told;
Another of those mysteries the Sacred Scriptures hold.

And if his shadow ceased to heal the sick and lame
Was Peter's faith in God still thought to be the same,
Or was he criticized by those who, seeking healing, came
And found a man who made no extraordinary claims?

And how did Peter feel about his shadow's impotence?
Did he long for "good old days" when he could sense
The presence of the "Mighty Hand of God" on him,
And feel the exhilaration of hundreds pressing in?

What was it like to live in the shadow of a shadow?
Did he ever wish that it would come again and show
The world that in his hand he held the prophet's rod;
That in his shadow - his mere shadow - he embodied God?

Or did he know, with a wisdom born of many years,
That "signs and wonders", though they're sought with tears,
And fervent prayers, are not the prophet's to command,
But given rather, for God's purpose,
                in His time, and from His hand.

On Faithlessness

Oh you of little faith,
You trust Me "not enough,"
But seek a miracle,
Demand a sign,
Require deliverance,
Ask for *forever* now.
I am Forever,
Eternal God,
Everlasting Father,
Alpha and Omega,
Resurrection and Life.
Whoever believes in Me,
Though he die,
Has *forever* now.

Righteousnesses

Awash in "righteousness",
   the world is bathed in blood.

A thousand righteousnesses,
   vying for supremacy,
   denying, by their bloody deeds
   the very gods they claim to serve,
   have aimed the world toward
   Apocalypse . . . an Armageddon.

Led, not by Righteousness,
   but selfishness,
   by fear, and human greed,
   we ride to Gog and Magog,
   upon a blood-red steed.

More Questions Than Time Allows

Time!
Just what is this thing
we call time?

Inexorable,
it yields to nothing,
caters to no one.

Mysterious!
Is it wave or particle,
or wholly immaterial?

Incalculable,
is it endless, or too infinitesimally
small to comprehend?

Omnipresent,
it opens and closes
all our doors.

Imminent,
it hides but never
goes away.

Immaterial,
it escapes all efforts to
contain it.

Generous,
it bestows a
thousand joys.

Perfect Imperfection

Ruthless,
it wrings the heart
with pain.

Ambivalent,
it gives and
takes way.

Fickle,
shortening every pleasure,
lengthening every pain.

Omnipotent,
it masters great
and small.

Patient,
it waits through
all eternities.

Inexplicable,
no language can
comprehend it.

Time!
What is this thing
we call time?

A God thing?
Or is it only known
to mortal man?

An earth thing?
Or will it last
for all eternities?

A good thing?
Or did it come because
we fell?

Can it "feed" us?
Or does it only make us
feel our hunger more?

Shall we embrace it?
Or would that embrace
destroy our soul?

Heel-Pullers

Madeleine L'Engle tells us
That the Jesus we grasp
May be very different from
The Jesus who grasps us.

It's true. Jacob, clinging to the angel,
Begging, in the darkness, to be blessed,
Had not guessed the hip-wrenching
Power of the Angel that he grasped.

The uneven gait, the searing pain,
That forever marked his steps,
Reminded Jacob daily
Of the "blessing" he had gained.

A Prayer for My Neighbor

Lord, your ways are beyond finding out.
Why should I, the blessings of life be given -
Health, clear mind, years of time? No doubt
That is one of the "secrets" you'll reveal in heaven.

I see others whose blessings - we all have them -
Seem fewer than mine; less full of Your care -
Short lives grown in poor soil and cut off at the stem -
More a blight than a blessing, they bear.

Oh, God let my sight be wrong - my judgment untrue -
Let the things that I "see" be not the things that are.
Let me see that the "blighted" are filled with You,
That they joy in their life, in spite of their scars.

I need to know, Lord, that you've not blessed me
Above others, though I seem so wonderfully blessed.
I ask not for less than you've willed there to be,
Only to know that others have more than I've guessed.

Your honor is at stake, Lord. I recall that you said
You are no respecter of persons, no favorites claim.
Be then to all men what you are to me - Lord aid
The afflicted that they may joy in Your Name.

Mortality

Mortal we are,
And we best not forget it
Lest we think we can build a tower
So high that it will over-top
The will and plans of God.

Three score and ten, God's gift to men,
And even that an average
Not yet achieved except
In privileged havens of health and wealth,
Called the "developed" world.

For every "good day" given into our life
One less remains to be given,
And when that gift of life is spent,
Sorry we will be if we have spent it all
In vain attempts to keep this dying life.

Countless Shades

Countless Shades there be that walk
The earth;
That stalk the birth
Of every human child,
And follow it
Through every human mile,
Until at last they sit
In triumph with their Shadow king
Who rules, he says,
O're everything.

They sit in triumph as they sing
His praise.
They flaunt the ways
Their hero-leader
Out maneuvers
The scorned, "savior-bleeder".
Fully confident, they know

Their captives,
Firmly held in stow,
Are their master's palliatives.

But they fail to sense the tremors
In the earth,
Caused by
Infant-Savior's birth;
Fail to note,
With time enough to act,
The words the prophets wrote.
So slowly, slowly, now
They feel the fear,
That their leader's doom is drawing near.

Countless shades there be that tremble
At the thought
That the captives will be brought
To the throne of Sentence-Reader,
Purchased by the death
Of Savior-Bleeder,
And their witness there
Will spell the Shadow's everlasting doom,
Sending Shadow, and his Shades into
An everlasting Godless tomb.

A Hill Far-away

There is a wooded trail
That winds its way around a mountain,
And all its lofty vistas never fail,
To snatch my breath.
For certain
It is God's highway,

A grand pathway
Leading to a meeting at its summit.
Was it here the worlds were called
Into their present form -
And from them torn
A single one,
A solitary designated sphere -
The only place in all the universe where
The need for Prophet Seer
Would require a promontory near,
A place where saving sounds would shear
The darkness, banish fear,
And draw the frightened, trembling masses there
To hear the news that peace on earth was near?

Balaam's Speaking Ass
(Numbers, Chapters 22 - 24)

I spoke in tongues today;
The Spirit came on me and helped me say
The words that turned my master from his foolish way.

I "spoke" one thing, God meant another,
I thought I spoke *my* mind but rather
It was God who spoke unto my master.
I spoke with words I had not learned;
With meanings I had not discerned,
But with a mind in which the Spirit burned.

Another, standing by, would say that I
Had simply brayed . . . and so would I;
That I had offered no advice.

But the words I spoke in native tongue
Were Spirit-born, and on them hung
The future of God's chosen ones;
Hebrews – sons of Abram's sons,
Through whom He'd send His Savior-Son.

Someday, perhaps, the Spirit-led
Will learn the meaning of the words they've said;
And see how, in the Spirit, they conveyed,
In tongues, or in some other way,
The truth that God had wished to say:
And how their tongues that seemed to them to only bray,
Were used to speak the very words of God that day.

Men Who Know What They Know

Men who have seen God face to face
Are not easy to look in the eye.
They are lit by a fire, easy to trace;
A confidence hard to come by.

They are world disturbers,
Men who have seen and heard
Things that shake the suburbs,
Breaking their streets and their curbs.

"These men have turned the world on its head!".
They objectively know what they know -
Their god is not dead -
And they lead all dead faiths in tow.

A Patriot's Prayer and A Response

God Bless America . . .
America The Beautiful . . .
America, Love it or Leave it . . .
Support our troops . . .
America, Land of Freedom . . .
America, The City on a Hill . . .
God love us all . . .

How do I love thee?
Let me count the ways.
I love you most when I can see
The love of justice in you streets.
When I can see humility,
Ability to confess your sins,
And turn from them,
And turn your hearts to me.
I've loved you to death, my death;
How much do you love me?

Ahasuerus's Sin

Ahasuerus must have thought
he honored Vashti with his request
that she appear - as one merely bought -
and preen at his behest.

I cheer for her and give her honor.
Though I don't know her motivation,
her refusal to be a mere "adorner"
raises her in my estimation.

Her defiant "No!" Struck a mighty blow
to the man-made rules
that make some "high" and others "low";
that make some "owners" and others "tools".

I don't depreciate her beauty
or her husband's "love" of it.
He may well have thought it duty
to share his prize with those with whom he'd sit.

But did he seek to honor her?
Did he make one living soul among them
know the depth of character
that made her beautiful to him?

Love By Demolition
(Mark 2:1 - 12)

Someday I'll need to fix that leaky roof.
A part of me knows it should be fixed,
But every drip of water, when it rains,
Reminds me of the day, and of the way,
It began to be a problem.

The audacity of those who made it leak
Still amazes me.
And their thoughtlessness in leaving it,
To celebrate their friend's healing,
Was the crowning piece.

I howled in indignation as they hammered through,
Spilling dirt and debris all over those beneath their blows;
Breaking dishes and endangering all below.

To no avail! No one cared a whit
For his own safety or that of my things.

Their focus was on a man,
A man come down from above
Through a gaping hole in heaven's canopy,
Let down, not to be healed, but to heal,
Not to break and scatter, but to be broken.

When all had gone their way and I was left
To clear away broken boards and scattered clay,
I turned to Him with angry words to say.
He smiled, looked through the ragged hole,
And through its portal, He began to pray.

Ah, Pharisee in me, how poorly do you see
The hand of God that ceaselessly
Tears the roof away, and thus displays
His love and power in ways
That leave insistent, dripping memories.

Supernova
(The Lonely Center)

It is lonely in the center these days.
Everyone has fled to the edges,
Thinking they've found truth there,
Or can create it if it isn't there already.
Time was when only the eccentric
Sought the edges,
Finding there a refuge from some truth
Their oblong souls could not endure,
A place so wide that eccentricity didn't matter;

Where their wobbling gait disturbed no one,
And each strident voice
Was like a tree, falling silent
In an uninhabited forest.
Now the edges have become
The common habitat
Where minorities
Declare themselves majorities;
Where their "common wisdom" seeks to define
"Common good" in terms that have a ring
Of selfishness about them,
My interest,
My benefit,
My vision,
My country,
My party,
My goals.
We speak of "left" and "right"
As though they define the "edges"
Of our world,
Unaware that a globe
Is made of infinite "edges",
Expandable,
As every eccentricity,
Every obstinacy,
Every righteousness,
Demands,
And is accorded,
Its place to wobble –
Or swagger and shout –
And all the while the center,
Lonely and depopulated,
Must preserve the "balance",
The gravity,
That will hold our world together,

Lest it implode and,
Like a dying supernova,
Inhale its edges,
Silencing forever,
All the strident voices.

Mixed Economies

I see their gilded images each night
And wonder at the height
They've reached.

In spinning, flashing, tumbling frames
They trumpet, without shame,
Their vaunted, bloated fame.

They promise us, though it's a lie,
That we need never see a leaden sky
If only, what they "sell", we'll buy.

Promises, these marketers of lies employ,
Of health, prestige, fulfillment, even joy,
To sell their latest, greatest "toy."

Broken "toys", they are, before they're made;
Hauled off to refuse heaps before their labels fade,
Leaving hollow, empty hearts to jade.

O God, will those who profit from such lies
Escape the consequences of their guise?
It seems I only see their profits rise.

But they are merchantmen - self-serving -
From one objective never swerving,
That the bottom-line is upward curving.

Oh God, may those who chose to bear your Name,
Be ever careful not to bring It shame
By claiming more than You would have them claim.

May they tell of a Kingdom, set apart;
Where paupers of the spirit make a start
Toward a Kingdom, not of wealth, but of the heart.

Thank you, Savoir, for showing us Your Father's way,
An economy of having all, and giving it away;
A "bottom-line" that, descending,
      crosses theirs and goes another way.

On Being Right

I've had occasion just now
To wonder about "being right".
I guess it really depends how
One means it; one might
Wish to be "right" even when wrong;
To be on the winning side
Of a struggle protracted too long
By selfishness, rancor, and pride.

Or, one might wish to be right
Even if it means "defeat";
Giving up one's own cherished light
To "retreat"
Into the truth.

Perfect Imperfection　　　　　　　The Prophet's Eye

Ah, that we would stubbornly cling
To love of the true,
Giving to everything
Its fair and appropriate due.

Righteous Father,
Make me persistent enough
To insist on the true –
To patiently wait to see it aright –
And then willingly grant it its due,
Foregoing insistence,
Fighting every desire
I have to be "right".

Let God be True . . .
And every man a liar!

Of Shepherds and Sheep

Shepherds, see your flock,
Ranged upon the hillsides,
Fed and sheltered and loved.
They live, heedless of the care
That you've bestowed on them.

Sheep were made for shepherds
And shepherds for sheep.
The loving interaction of
Caregiver
And cared for
Is lovely to the eyes of God.

Shepherds, you've tended to the wounds
Of the flock, pouring the oil of compassion
On their open sores, binding them up,
Strengthening and protecting the weak
Against the bullying of the bold,
Planning for their every need.

Oh Shepherds, a storm is brewing,
Sweeping in from the sea.
Gather the flock, find the stragglers,
Bring them into the shelter
Of the sheepfold
Away from the ravages of wind and rain.

Hurry Shepherds! There is no time to lose,
There are eyes in the darkness,
Gaping mouths and snarling voices.
Those who love the sheep, only to devour them,
Are circling in the dark,
About to claim some wayward prey.

Be quick Shepherds! They are among us!
In the darkness it is hard to see,
Hard to tell.
What is sheep and what is not.
They snatch the young and hound the weak,
The sheep wound each other in their confusion.

Fight Shepherds! Charge! Your sheep are at risk!
With voice, and sticks, and stones,
In front and back and on every side,
Flail and shout and curse and tear
At the enemies of your flock
Until they turn and run away.

Search Shepherds! Search, in the darkness
Of a storm that seems to have no end.
Tune your ear to hear,
Amid the wail of wind,
And snarl of foe,
The cry of wounded lambs.

Find them, Shepherds!
Bring them, torn and trembling.
Enfold them in your care,
Binding wounds
And soothing fears
Until they sleep a healing sleep.

It is morning, Shepherds. See your flock,
Ranged upon the hillsides,
Fed and sheltered and loved.
They forget the storm, forget the snarling wolves,
Forget, even, that the Shepherds cast their lives
Before their mortal foes.

Oh Shepherds, you are wounded!
The wind has worn you down.
The wolves have torn your flesh.
You gasp for breath
And cling to broke reeds
To keep from falling.

Come away, Shepherds.
Leave the flock in the care of others
Whom the Master Shepherd will send.
Come away and be healed.
Come away and be healed.
Come away and be healed.

At the End of the World

We stand, perpetually,
At the end of the world.
There is no other place to stand.
But slowly we sense
That this is not Apocalypse,
Not Armageddon, not Gog nor Magog,
Not even a Rapture.
We are all "left behind".

Crowded here,
At the end of time,
We shuffle for space,
Vie for attention,
Fight and die for trivialities,
Called wealth, fame,
Pleasure, comfort,
Health, possessions.

We peer into the Abyss
Called Future,
But cannot, dare not,
Go there.
We turn to examine
The Past
And find it filled with
Confusing mists.

And so we pivot
On our tiny plot of now-ness,
Unable to see ahead,
Unable to see behind,
Unwilling to admit
That this place,

At the end of the world,
Is man's appointed home.

Sorry the man,
The woman,
Who knows not that
A home is to be lived in;
A place of love,
Security, contentment;
A place to put down roots
And raise a family.

Voice to Voice

I'm not afraid to hear what you have to say,
I need to hear it if I'm to understand you.
Why do you resist my thoughts and turn away?
Do my words have less right than your words do?

Do you really see "evil" in the things I espouse?
Tell me, with specificity, what it is you see,
And why it is so wicked as to arouse
A fear in you; a desire to do away with me?

In a fallen world, fear is the armor every creature wears.
It isn't the sole reserve of humans;
The fiercest beast is fiercest when he fears,
The meekest hare turns tail in fear and runs.

What is it from which fear runs?
What, that fear fears most?
The unknown, of course, some blinding sun,
Some uncharted, darkly wooded coast.

An eclipse, a strange and sudden sound,
A language never heard before,
A face that's strangely long, not round,
A moving shadow that you can't ignore.

But fear can be contained, controlled,
Even abolished, by perception.
Shadows lose their fearsome hold,
When light dispels their apprehension.

So why not let some "light" into our conversation?
Words, speech, explanation, are the lights
That illuminate the path of civil-ization,
Voice to voice, and giving every voice its rights.

A Defining Issue: What Is Pentecostal?

This question of who is Pentecostal,
    and who isn't, is troublesome.

I'm finding that those who profess
    to value a Pentecostal "service",
    don't share the same definition
    of what makes a gathering "Pentecostal."

I suppose the infamous song,
    "You Can't Have Church Until the Holy Ghost
    Shows Up," is an attempt to define it.

But how does one know when the Holy Ghost has shown up?

Is it when all the pews in the church are full,
    or when the choir is "rocking,"
    or when the saints are dancing in the aisles,

or when the decibels reach ear-damaging levels,
or when there is frothy-mouthed preaching,
or when an emotionally moving "video" is displayed,
or when a "special speaker" moves the saints
    to give great sums for a good cause,
or when someone gives a message in tongues
    or a prophecy,
or when the altars are flooded with people?

Or is it when one saint takes the hand of another
    whom they sense is in distress,
    or when one is moved to give their last dollar
        to support a missionary in a far off land,
    or when a teacher in the Beginner Sunday School class
        wipes the nose of a tiny tyke
        and teaches her or him to sing, "Jesus Loves Me",
    or when a bag of groceries is purchased anonymously
        to aid a hungry family,
    or when a believer quietly prays for those
        who lead our nation or our church?

Or is it ALL or ANY of these things?

When did the Holy Spirit subject Himself
    to the will of man?
Who is qualified to know His purposes,
    to determine his timing,
    to declare his message,
    to propose his methods,
    to critique his "performance",
    to declare him "present" or "absent"?

Can one person define "Pentecostal" for another;
    declare one "spiritual" and another not,

        based on arbitrary, external evidences?

Can one local body of believers define
        what "Pentecostal" will look like
        in another body?

Father in Heaven, we (your Church) need
        a baptism in the Holy Spirit;
We need a rebirth
        of love, one for another,
        of faith, one in the other,
        of concern, one for the other,
        of desire, to serve,
                and not critique
                each other,
        of acceptance of the diverse gifts
                you distribute among us,
        of joy, in the gifts of the other.

Name Bearers
(Revelation 2:17)

We are name-bearers, every one,
Marked by the course we choose,
Daughters all, and sons,
Fathered (named) by the mundane things
        we love, then lose.

Oh, to bear a name we cannot lose,
To be a son or daughter, known
And claimed by Him who views us
As His child; our name inscribed forever
        on a pure white stone.

The Storm

Annie was not a perfect lamb.
Born of good stock,
To a good dam,
But no credit to the flock.

Her limbs were thin and weak,
Her wool was coarse and bad,
Her manner, shy and meek.
A "heart" was all that Annie had.

Two men owned the flock
And daily led them out to pasture.
Some sheep, to one, would flock,
Some followed close the other master.

On "What to do with Annie,"
The men sharply differed.
She had no value as a sheep
And often was a hazard.

The first to catch a blight,
And prone to pass it on.
Prone as well to fright
When storms were coming on.

 "Get rid of her" one man said, "See,
She only draws the scavengers."
"But notice how she follows me,"
The other said, "I have a love for her."

Perfect Imperfection

So Annie learned which one to trust,
And chose each day to follow him.
The other, watching in disgust,
Vowed, someday, to sever them.

His chance came on a stormy night,
When wind and rain and darkness
Sent the sheep, in frightened flight,
In search of their respective masters.

But Annie, true to form, got lost.
"No loss!" laughed her tormentor,
"Leave her for wolves to come across.
They'll make a tasty meal of her."

But the good shepherd began to weep;
He could not leave it there.
Though, of little value as a sheep,
Annie had a "heart" that made him care.

So out in blackness of the storm
The shepherd ventured forth,
Seeking any sign of Annie's form;
By seeking, giving Annie worth.

The anti-shepherd ventured out as well,
Determined to find Annie first.
His intention – born and bred in hell –
To kill what, to the shepherd, had great worth.

Both men made their shepherd calls,
And Annie heard them both.
But storm and fright combined to make it all
A blur to Annie, sheltered in the undergrowth.

Perfect Imperfection The Prophet's Eye

She thought she heard her shepherd's voice,
And started moving toward it.
But then another said, "Annie, I'm your choice.
Don't let that false voice draw you to it."

Annie heard no words that night –
None her sheep-brain comprehended –
Only sounds . . . and which was right?
Which voice good, and which one bad, intended?

Both voices called to come to them,
Both voices spoke with gentle urgency.
And Annie's "sheep-sense" deep within,
Tried to weigh, to know, their authenticity.

If Annie could only see the men,
Could hear, without the storm, their voice
Then she would know which one of them
Was true, and she would make her choice.

Annie longed to hear some certain sound,
To see some certain thing;
She craned her weary neck around
To hear, and peered through driving rain.

She saw a form, a shadow, with its hand extended,
Heard a sound that seemed to say,
"Come, Annie. Come. Your trial is ended.
Come! I'll save you. Come this way."

The words were only sounds to her,
Sounds she'd never heard before.
But spoken in such gentle tones and near,
She turned and moved to hear some more.

Then, another shadow turned her 'round;
She heard a voice she'd heard before,
She heard a phrase, the single sound
Her "heart" was seeking for.

"I love you, Annie, as all my sheep, I do.
For you – for all my sheep – I'd die."
The only non-sheep word that Annie knew
The shepherd used to draw her nigh.

The anti-shepherd left in full defeat.
Deception he could speak with fluency,
But *one word*, his mouth would not repeat –
Love! A word that sheep interpret instantly.

Jehovah-Rapha

Lord, if you had been here . . .
        my brother,
        my mother,
        I, would not have died!

But I was there, I Am.
        I Am the Lord that healeth thee.

I formed the DNA
        that fights the blight,
        that forms the scab,
        that filters blood,
        and cools the fevered brow.

I hid gifts of healing in
> the food you eat,
> the air you breathe,
> the ground you till,
> the sleep you sleep.

I give wisdom to the mind of man,
> skill to the surgeon's hands,
> healing in a nurse's care,
> guidance to those who seek
> to find a cure.

And they brought to Him their sick,
> obese but eating still more,
> flaccid but seeking more ease,
> malignant but chain smoking still,
> fried but championing legalization,
> diseased but enthralled with sex,
> depressed but feeding on husks.

And they said to Him, "Lord, if you will,
> you can make us whole."

And He said, "This is my body?
> This is the Temple of the God?
> My house is a house of life,
> but you have made it a house of death.
> If you would be healed
> give up you self-seeking ways
> and eat the bread I gave to you."

And they turned away sad
> for they loved their ways
> more than life.

On Democracy

We hear much about discontent these days,
Much about those who hate the way
Government runs or, in their view,
The way it hinders them from running.

They are anti-Government we're told.
Throw the bums out, put "Sarah" in their place!
Without knowing what "Sarah" stands *for*
They see in her a champion for all they are *against.*

But discernible in all their rhetoric and racket
Is a theme the media has failed to see.
It's simple; they are opposed to the principal
That duly elected governments have legitimacy.

They are opposed to *being governed.*
They want to say whatever they wish to say
About anyone they wish to harm,
In any way they wish to say it, facts be damned!

Their god is *liberty*, not for all, but for themselves,
Liberty to *pack heat* in overheated venues,
Liberty to bray with overheated invective
Against those who seek to extend liberty to all.

They wave the flag but dishonor the principles it stands for.
They invoke their god as an ally in their intolerance.
They raise self-interest to the level of the sacred.
They make opposition the badge of responsibility.

Perfect Imperfection   The Prophet's Eye

They claim descent from noble forefathers
But miss a crucial distinction; those forefathers
Rebelled against a tyranny that made them pay
But refused to let them "play"; taxation but no vote.

Our modern rebels are mad, of all things,
Not because they can't vote but because they lost.
They are upset because, in losing, they are required
To give someone else's idea a chance to prove its worth.

They fail to see a critical reality,
That freedom is fragile; too fragile
To endure, for long, their intolerance.
Words become actions – actions have consequences.

Consequences do not bear party labels;
They help or harm without distinction
Of race, or religion, or party affiliation;
They lash *back* as well as lash *out*.

God bless America! Yes, we all hope for that.
But God help America too, to be *one* nation,
Under God, with liberty and justice, not just
For the loudest and most angry, but for all.

A Final Word

Let us measure success . . .
Or rather, let us find a tool,
A way to reach consensus,
By . . . by . . . by some unfailing rule.

Where can we find a true metric,
The unerring guide to approbation,
The definitive yardstick
Marked with perfect calibrations?

Numbers? Ah, there is an unfailing guide!
Fans, customers, adherents, denote success.
Numbers can't be brushed aside.
They provide the truest test.

Dollars? Dollars, bring fame and honor,
Allowing great structures to rise,
Enterprises to flourish, luxuries to savor,
Institutions to laud and to prize.

Acclaim? Yes! Headlines that trumpet;
Masses that gather in stadia
To shout, wave, and parrot
The credenda *ad nauseam*.

Respect? Ah, joy! Seats in high places,
Name recognition – voices lowered
In honor, and turned faces
As tributes and credits are showered.

Power? Of course. Power to elect
And power to depose,
The powerful gather to select,
Convene to dispose.

These are the regalia of winners,
The proud emblems of success,
Turning the deeds of rank sinners
To unquestioned righteousness.

Unquestioned success? Yes,
By those being lauded,
And those who seek access
To those thus applauded.

Basking in a moment of cheap glory,
Adorned with some badge of success,
They forget that all fame is aleatory,
Coming and going at no one's behest.

Except . . . unless . . . until
One's fame is fairly won,
Declared, bestowed and sealed
By an Eternal "Child, well done!"

Forgiveness

You say your heart is black;
That you might never turn it back
To one whose arrogance, displayed,
Brought harm to those you love,
Or sent them to their grave.

Perhaps you know your heart;
Perhaps it is your weaker part;
Unwilling to forgive an injury so grave.
If so, I pray it will be trained
By One who facing such, forgave.

But I know your heart somewhat;
Know enough to say it's got
A huge vault of forgiveness -
Mercies that you've learned
From Him whose dying heart,
To save us, yearned.

This Is My Body
(A Poem-song)

With hands that are trembling I lift the bread,
Destined and willing to die in your stead,
Your sorrow – my sorrow, I take on my head.
My body – your body, given instead.

Chorus:
This is my body - given to you,
Symbol and substance,
Eternally True.
Broken yet whole; dying yet living,
Ever my Body; needing yet giving,
This is my body - given to you.

The children are coming, forbid them not,
The Kingdom is theirs, and what they have got -
Their simple - their joyful - their unfettered faith,
Is the key that unlocks the heavenly gate.

Chorus:

They are my body - given to you,
Symbol and substance,
Eternally True.
Broken yet whole; dying yet living,
Ever my Body; needing yet giving,
This is my body - given to you.

The hungry are here, begging for food,
Shepherdless flocks; tattered and rude,
Insisting, demanding, their right to be fed
Your fishes, your loaves of God-given bread.

Chorus:

They are my body - given to you,
Symbol and substance,
Eternally True.
Broken yet whole; dying yet living,
Ever my Body; needing yet giving,
This is my body - given to you.

Strangers are here, pounding the gate,
Illiterate hordes, coming too late,
Without home, without peace, or knowledge of Me;
I am peace, I am home, bring them to me.

Chorus:
They are my body - given to you,
Symbol and substance,
Eternally True.
Broken yet whole; dying yet living,
Ever my Body; needing yet giving,
This is my body - given to you.

Bridge:
What you do to these, you do to me too.
Listen . . . my body is speaking to you –
Eat of my flesh, drink my blood too,
Share in my death and I'll live in you.
This is my body – given to you.
This is my body – given to you.

Pentecost

What happened on that day - that Pentecost -
That echoes as a song, not lost,
But ever building t'ward a coming day,
That human tongues can only hope to say?

The Paraclete - the Ezer-gift - The Promised One
Was sent to represent the Son;
To lift Him up in power for all to see,
So He can show His Father faithfully.

The Church was born again in Living Flame
That, leaping up, proclaimed the name
Of God the Father, God the Son,
And told works that they had done.

The Spirit of the Father and Spirit of the Son,
Drawing men together, uniting them as one,
To carry to the world an everlasting joy;
A treasure of great price, a gold without alloy.

Oh Spirit of the living God, come fill your Church today,
And send us out, inflamed by you, into our daily way,
To loft the Name of Christ by tongue and deed
O're those whom you would visit in their need.

Parallel Lives: Inversely Related

From heaven to earth they came.
With the brightness of heavenly flame,
Angels falling, and angels who sang,
Attend their arrival, and their leaving again.

Perfect Imperfection 　　　　　　　The Prophet's Eye

Shining with his highest glory,
Speaking high angelic oratory,
Whispering words, conspiratory,
Claiming for himself a terra-tory.

Standing in the Holy Place,
Gazing on the Holy Face,
Luring others to his mace,
Defiling the angelic race.

Banned from heaven's life,
Choosing Geos for a wife,
Bearing sons whose lives are rife
With unfettered hell-bound strife;

Blinding, so they cannot see
The source of all their misery;
Binding, through eternity
With his chains of prideful enmity.

Eternally the same,
Bearing Sonship in his name,
Laying all aside to claim
Servanthood and feel no shame.

Bowing to his Father's will,
Son Divine, but willing still
To lay aside those powers until
A saving work He could fulfill.

Exiled from His heavenly home,
Choosing flesh he strayed not from
His mission to become
Savior to each flesh-bound one.

Dying first, He then arose,
Claiming victory o're His foes,
Taking back His royal roles,
Eternal Son, eternal life bestows

From heaven to earth they came.
With the brightness of heavenly flame,
Angels falling, and angels who sang,
Attend their arrival, and their leaving again.

Images

Images! Thank God for all the images!
They've served us now for long, long ages,
Letting us take precious hostages
Of thoughts and deeds and messages;
Filling out our languages
With precious picture packages
That bring to mind the human passages
Through which our race now forages,
Hoping those it salvages
Can be the healing bandages
That cure our self-inflicted damages.

Oh God, who speaks to us in images,
Who, through Your Son, once did and does,
Speak now again. Yea, speak again to us,
In "tongues" our minds can grasp indigenous.

Redemption

What makes us think we are more important to God
Than all the rest of his creation?
I have some guesses, if you'll allow.

First, being *able* to "think" – an intelligent clod,
Blessed with powers of articulation –
We arrogantly rank ourselves "first" and put all else below.

Then there's that thing about sin and redemption.
Surely God must love most
His prodigal "sons", his wayward sheep;

Rather than exercise His right of ademption,
He has chosen, we are told, at great personal cost,
To forgive them, and return them, safe to the keep.

Surely we can draw the conclusion,
From all this activity,
That Father loves us more than the rest;

More than our inarticulate brethren
Whose apparent impassivity
We read as evidence of their worth-less-ness.

But is it true? Do our speechless fellow creatures
Not groan under the burden
Imposed on them by our prodigality?

Animate or inanimate, near or far, man fractures
The peace of their garden,
Tearing, and killing, and consuming rapaciously,

Perfect Imperfection   The Prophet's Eye

As though the hills and valleys and lakes and streams,
And that which lives in them,
Were not also made at God's command,

As though His ear does not hear the groans and screams
In the oceans condemned
To drown in the wastes of prodigal man.

Lest you think it too naïve
To give a voice
To voicelessness, to "lifelessness",

Hear the heart of ancients grieve,
Giving voice . . .
Voice and ***hope*** to hopelessness.

"How long will the land lie parched
        and the grass in every field be withered?
Because those who live in it are wicked,
        the animals and birds have perished."[*]

"We know that the whole creation has been groaning
        as in the pains of childbirth
        right up to the present time."[**]

"The creation waits in eager expectation
        for the sons of God to be revealed . . .
        in **hope** that [it] will be liberated
        from its bondage and decay
        and brought into the glorious freedom
               of the children of God."[***]

The sons of Adam came to steal, kill and destroy.
The sons of God, we are told, will come
To bring life, and to bring it more abundantly.†

But in *this time*, when Adam's sons are earth's viceroy,
Could we not share this glorious home
With deeper love and greater care for all God's progeny?

---

*   Jeremiah 12:4
**   Romans 8:22
***   Romans 8:19-21
†   An adaptation of Jesus' words quoted in John 10:10

Heart's Ease: The Home of Heart

We hear a lot about homelessness even in an affluent society like that of the United States. But no one is truly homeless. Some may sadly spend their days on a sidewalk grate where a little warmth issues from the nearby buildings but even that becomes a "home", a turf for which its "owner" will often fight and die.

Home is where we find a sense of being. The more it is effused with love and security the more it nourishes our humanity. The closer it is built to resemble our *original home* the more it becomes a place of "heart's ease". I was blessed, in my infancy and youth, to know such a home. Not an affluent home; quite the opposite. But a home that my mind and heart continually returns to for comfort and nourishment long after its residents have scattered. And for the last 53 years I have been working, with the aid of my dear wife, Alice, to establish such a home for our children to remember. I could not have built such a home alone; Alice's constant faith and persistent love has been essential glue that holds our home together.

This section of poems, celebrating faith, is dedicated to my wife of 53 years, Alice Dawn (Nichols) Rapp

What is the Shape of Joy?

What is the shape of joy?
Does it come in a brightly colored box
Like the latest fad or toy?

What shape does joy take?
Is it large, like a new house
Overlooking a diamond lake?

Is joy made by great success?
Does it only come when our prayers
Get answered, "Yes"?

How can one be sure it is joy
That fills one's heart and breast
And not some cheap alloy?

Joy is not a "thing" but rather
A choiceful reshaping of our hearts;
Into which joy can gather.

Joy, then, is a heart shaped choice;
Made in the shape of our Father's will.
Try it, my friend, and rejoice!

Morning's Soft Light

All things are more beautiful in morning's soft light;
The drabbest of scenes, scarred by man's blight
Of "toys" and discards, hidden by shadows all night,
Is given, in morning's soft light,
                more charm than its right.

Psalm 99
(Loosely Translated – Song Lyrics)

The God whom I worship is King of the Earth,
He is Lord of the place where I live.
He is Great and Awesome, Holy and Just,
Faithful and quick to forgive,

He is worthy of praise,
Worthy of praise,
Holy and worthy of praise
He is worthy of praise,
Worthy of praise,
Holy and worthy of praise

I'll Rise on His Love
(A Song)

When I am weary and my spirit is weak,
And my faith seems a reed in the wind.
When doubts cloud my mind
Like an ominous storm,
Shrouding my spirit with in,
Then I'll turn to the One who can calm every storm,
Lord Jesus, come lift me again.

Then I'll rise on the strength of His undying love,
I'll soar on the wings of His mercy,
He'll call me to come to His marvelous throne,
And rest in the fold of his arms,
He'll call me to come to His marvelous throne,
And rest in the fold of his arms,

When shadows grow long and the day is o're,
And my work is nearly done.
When earth-light grows dim
And heaven is bright,
Blazing a path to the sun,
Then I'll turn to the One who is always near,
Lord Jesus come lift me again.

He'll say, "Rise on the strength of my undying love.
Soar on the wings of my mercy.
Come little child to my marvelous home
And rest in the fold of my arms.
Come little one, to my marvelous home
And rest in the fold of my arms.

You may rise on the strength of His undying love,
You may soar on the wings of His mercy.
He calls you to come to His marvelous throne
And rest in the fold of his arms.
Come little ones, to His marvelous throne
And rest in the fold of his arms.

Sharing Joy!

I often find a joy when least expected,
Lying at my feet or in my heart.
At times a thing, at first rejected,
Newly seen, can make me start
To know the joy of it, and then,
Because I know the joy of it,
I take to a friend,
Put it in their heart,
And see if it will fit.

Sunday Morning "Him" Singing

Sunday morning is a time when friends
From every part of town begin
Their preparations to again
Join hearts and hands and voices in
Their praise.
With song and hymn
They honor God
      and lift a swell of praise to Him.

Heart's Ease: The Home of Heart

I come to you my Father King
And do the only thing
That being in your presence
Will allow; I rush to you and fling
Myself into your arms;
I press my head into your chest
And there upon the Holy Ark
I put my ear between the Cherubim
And rest.
I listen to the faithful beat
Of your Father-heart
And name this hollowed place
Wherein we meet,
Heart's Ease: The Home of Heart.

A Prayer for June 3, 2005

To shine so brightly, Lord;
To be a precious, golden hoard
Of goodness where you've stored
Eternal worth that I, in poverty, could not afford.

To share that bounty
With joy, and not a sense of duty;
To give as You have given me,
Riches freely taken, given now as generously.

The Servant's Prayer

We sometimes think the muses
        speak only to our spirits
        and that only artists
        can commune with them.
.

But we all have eyes,
        and ears, and skin,
        and tongues, and noses,
        each a gift, capable of
        teaching us,
        correcting us,
        inspiring us.

The sculptor sees in the stone
        what he needs to know
        to make a work of art.

The potter feels in the clay
        the pot or plate
        it wants to become.

The composer hears
        in the timbre of the horn
        the notes that must be
        assigned to it.

Lord make all your servants artists,
> saying, "May it be to me
> as You have said."

Give us all, in every task and duty,
> a desire to create
> something inspired.

Let the egg I fry instruct me
> when to turn it,
> how to make it "manna"
> for the one it feeds.

Let the face of the child I teach
> draw from me, words
> she needs to hear,
> so she can learn.

Let the brick I lay
> show me how to turn it,
> making it a perfect compliment
> to all its fellow bricks.

When I sweep
> let the broom, the floor,
> the furnishings,
> the purpose of the room,
> teach me how to sweep.

When I comfort
> let the eyes, the voice,
> the body tell me
> what will bring
> the greatest comfort.

When I must criticize –
>   when it is my duty to –
>   may my words be words
>   that shape a better world.

The tasks you give me, Lord,
>   will teach me
>   if I let them,
>   inspire me, even.

They will show me possibilities,
>   ways to bless the ones I serve,
>   adding "the artist's touch"
>   to all I do and say.

A Hymn

The heavens declare your glory -
The earth is your image displayed -
Together they blazon the story
Of wonders your hands have made.

Riding the rays of the morning -
Descending like dew from above -
Closing the day with the evening -
Enfolding us thus, in your love.

The thunderclaps speak of your power,
The lightning shows us your face,
Flashing its beams through the shower,
Inscribing your name with it's trace.

The stars in the depths of the heavens
Are messengers speaking in tongues,
Bringing your word to the millions
In languages never yet sung.

Who can gaze on the marvelous glories
Of all that your hands have wrought,
And not be moved to tell stories
With God-thoughts and mysteries fraught?

The fool denies your existence,
Rejecting all that he sees,
But a child, offering no resistance,
Quickly and humbly believes.

As a child let me stand at the mid-night,
Or at noon under bright blazing sun;
Let me see you, O God, with a child's sight,
And give praise for all you have done.

A Prayer for Friday, February 11, 2005

When the shades are pulled
They seem to say,
"Enough of good and ill we've culled
To to make of this one day."

We'll borrow not from what's ahead,
What's past is gone,
We've traveled where our hearts have led
And now we stand alone.

Dear God, take all that we have done
As unto you,
And things we did not do
Are things we'll leave with you.

The Perfect Day

What makes the day go as we wish it to?
We sometimes think it is the things we choose to do,
Especially so, attractions rare or new.
But deep lie the "wishes" I'm referring to,
Unspoken "wishes", oft ignored in lieu
Of louder ones that shout to be attended to.
What makes the day go as we wish it to?
At end of day, it is the things we always knew –
Work well done,
  a friend well served,
    and sensing God near you.

You Are Joy!
(Song Lyrics)

You are Joy, Lord,
You are Joy!
You are Joy, Lord,
You are Joy!

Coming from the fountain,
Rushing down the mountain
Is your matchless grace;
Filling all my spirit,
Every time I'm near it,
Lord, I seek your face.

You are Joy, Lord,
You are Joy!
You are Joy, Lord,
You are Joy!

A Samaritan Leper's Song
(Luke 17:11-19)

The word crept near,
From who knows where,
That there was hope at hand
For our desperate outcast band.

Hope is the last thin string
To which the hopeless cling;
A snatching at the air
In case there's something there.

We stood at law's distance
Seeking, hoping, Love's assistance.
Love sent us away . . . sent us away
Saying, "Go and let the priest assay!"

But as we went,
As we were sent,
A gush of healing, fresh,
Flowed through my dying flesh.

Healed I was,
And all because
Love sent me on my way,
Saying, "Go and let the priest assay!"

And I alone,
A mere Samaritan
Who had no temple priest to cleanse him,
Turning, ran to Jesus once again.

Hearing Love's insistence;
Approaching at love's close distance,
There I let *my Priest* assay,
For he had washed my filth away.

Good morning!

Morning does not begin,
As many are wont to think,
When their alarm sets off a din
And they brush at the bathroom sink.
That may be "morning" to them,
But not the morning of which I think.

Morning is one of God's gifts.
Made in those earliest days,
It comes to enlighten and lifts
The darkness that swirls and sways
Around us in mountainous drifts,
Obscuring our perilous ways.

It needs no alarm to signal its rise;
Waiting in darkness,
It will always surprise
Those who, with unerring preciseness
Command its coming; and vainly arise,
Calling their rising the nighttime's demise.

Ah, come with me to a woodless hill,
And we will see the morning near.
For in the darkness dank and still
Morning waits 'til it can hear
Its Maker's call, and at His will
Light will break, shadows flee,
      and day be here.

In All Things Give Thanks

All things have a beginning and an end.
Of some we dread the beginning
And seek to somehow deftly bend
Their course in hopes of winning
Respite from their chilling wind.

Of some we cannot wait to start
And hope the end will never come;
Faithless, we, and hard of heart,
Assuming it would mis-become
The Father, to another blessing start.

Oh, Lord, may every thing
You bring into my life,
Though it bless or sorely sting,
Be received with humble joy, rife
With praises that I sing.

Four Words
(John 3:16)

Four words
Bring freedom to the world.
The Father looked toward
Our captive race and hurled
The words that broke our cords,
When on a cross, unfurled,
He wrote the words,
"I love you, world!"

Sunday Graces

Sunday graces
Come in many forms;
In lovely hearts and faces
In which the love of Christ is born.

How Will We Praise Him?

I wonder if, some future day,
Some thing will take the place
Of words we use; some way
Be found to tell the grace
That human tongues are wont say.

Or will our words be enlarged, with space
Enough that they can hold and tell
The awesome beauty of God's face;
Will they then be capable, as well,
Of describing all His matchless benefice?

A Sunday Morning Prayer

Precious hearts-within-my-heart,
We rise again this day to start
Anew our praise, and do our simple part,
By sending forth, on man-made cart,
A man-made Ark of God;
Another human start
To bring into His presence
Our wayward stubborn hearts.

Oh come again Shekinah, sought;
Oh come and rest within our thoughts,
And take abode between the cherubim;
And make the gifts that lie within,
The life, the law, the living Bread,
Our food this day that lies ahead.

Come Lord
(For A Pastor Friend at A Difficult Hour)

A heavy heart is hard to bear.
Sometimes I wonder, Lord, how you bore it.
Earth-ness? God-ness?
Which informed your heart
As sorrow pressed upon it?

My heart has only earth-ness as its aid,
Unless you bring your God-ness to it.
Oh Lord of suffering, Lord of pain,
Is it too much to ask
    That you would come again;
Be born again in me,
    And help me bear my pain?

Patience

Lord, I thank you for the questions;
They draw me to your heart and mind.
The answers I can wait for –
Must wait for –
Even though a multitude of Answerers
Ply me with their certitude.

Let Everything That Hath Breath Praise Him

Some have claimed that God does not exist,
And some have called Him mute,
But even those who think Him dead persist
In ways that show their "faith" not absolute.

They swear by Him in anger or in need,
And often when occasion calls
They find a way, within their creed,
To speak His name in public halls.

I'm glad for every way His name is shown,
For every use of it proclaims Him real.
And deep within the marrow of his bones
The scoffer, even in his scoffing, bears His seal.

But oh, that all who speak His name
Would speak with faith-filled words,
But better yet, in faith-full ways, proclaim
Him real through deeds done other-ward.

The Gift of Time

There is no other gift like time.
It forms the queue in which
All other gifts must march in line;
No exceptions, no opportunities to switch.

It is time that bounds the gift of life,
And makes us cry, "Too short!"
When days, with joy are rife,
"Too long!" when they are filled with hurt.

It is time that gives,
And time that takes away;
Time it is that, as through a leaky sieve,
Retrieves its gifts at ending of each day.

Oh Father, in this time You've given me,
May I snatch a gift from Time's rich queue
And make of it the thing it's meant to be,
A gift that I will give again, well used, to You.

A Prayer

Give me a minute, Lord,
And I will praise you with it.
Give me an hour
And I will return a tithe to you.
Give me a year, Lord,
And you will see me once a week,
      Except on holidays.
Give me a lifetime
And I will seek you in my need.
Oh Lord, give me a lifetime . . .
      One minute at a time.

Martha's Complaint
(John 11:21-25)

Lord, if You had been here . . .
I sent for you, Lord,
      and you did not come!
Why did you tarry?
Didn't you know my fear?
Didn't you feel my heart breaking?

Dear Child, I am on a journey . . .
Going to a place where every fear
        and every sorrow meets.
If you but knew . . .
Knew the fear surrounding *Me,*
The death awaiting *Me*!

But Lord, if You had been here . . .
You knew I was weeping,
        and ignored my tears.
Why didn't you hurry?
Did you not care?
Were my pains nothing to you?

Dear Child, I am on a journey . . .
Going to a place where every hope
        and every joy is born.
Don't you know . . .?
I am the Resurrection and the Life.
Believe in Me and you will never die!

A Path to Joy

When some men hate you
        you may have found the path to righteousness.

When most men hate you
        you are more likely on the way that saints have trod.

When nearly all men hate you
        you have found the way to joy, through Golgotha.

Blessed are ye, when men shall hate you,

> *and when they shall separate you from their*
> *company, and shall reproach you, and cast out*
> *your name as evil, for the Son of man's sake.*
>
> *Rejoice ye in that day, and leap for joy:*
> > *for, behold, your reward is great in heaven:*
> > *for in the like manner did their fathers*
> > *unto the prophets.*
>
> (Luke 6:22 & 23 Authorize Version)

A Grain of Mustard Seed
(A meditation on Faith)

And Jesus said unto them . . If ye have faith
as a grain of mustard seed, ye shall say
unto this mountain, Remove hence to yonder place;
and it shall remove . . . Authorized Version

How much faith is "as" a mustard seed,
        and to what, about the seed,
        is faith compared;
        its size, its weight
        or its composition?
Who has weighed faith;
        measured it,
        found its physical properties
        and compared them
        to those of a mustard seed?

Hope, better called "little faith,"
        ventures forth timorously,
        investing little, trusting "luck",
        loosing as often as it wins.

When Jesus spoke of "little faith"
    and "great faith"
    it wasn't as a measure;
    little faith always failed,
    great faith moved "mountains."

Faith can't really be measured at all;
    it isn't a matter of *more* or *less*,
    bigger or *smaller;*
    faith either *is* or *isn't.*

If it *isn't*, then no mountains will move.

Faith *isn't* when it is based on mere hope;
    on desperate desire,
    misguided assumptions,
    manipulative hype,
    or poor doctrine.

Faith *isn't* when it
    promotes self-aggrandizement,
    is used as a prop to uphold
    a "tradition" of faith,
    ignores the will of the Father.

Faith *is* the absence of doubt;
    it comes by hearing
    and hearing
    and hearing
    the Word of God.

Faith *can* move mountains . . .
    if it is an expression of God's will;
    if God wants the mountain moved.

Faith is a servant, not of human desire,
> but of God's will;
> the vehicle by which the Will of God
> is done on earth as it is in heaven.

Faith senses – hears, sees and knows –
> the will of the Father,
> and tells the mountain,
> "Oh mountain,
> hear the will of the Lord,
> 'Be removed!'"

Faith comes not only by *hearing*,
> heart-*hearing*,
> spirit-*hearing*,
> but then by trusting
> what is heard.

Faith is a noun that requires an object:
> it sees the Father acting,
> hears the Father speak,
> and declares, *on earth*,
> what it sees *in heaven*.

Whatever you bind or loose on earth
> will be what you have seen
> bound or loosed in heaven.

Therefore, what you see bound
> or loosed in heaven,
> by faith, bind it, or loose it
> on earth.

One day faith may say to the mountain,
    "Be removed and cast into the sea."
One another it may say, "Don't stand around waiting
    for the mountain to move; rent a bulldozer
    and move it."

One day faith may say to sick man,
    "In the Name of Jesus Christ of Nazareth,
    rise up and walk!"
On another it may say, "drink no longer water,
    but take a little wine
    for your stomach's sake
    and your frequent infirmity."

Faith always prays, "*Your* kingdom come,
    Your will be done,
    on earth as it is in heaven."

Grace

We've figured out that to a large extent
God sends his gifts housed in a human tent;
That the fabric is not saved from rents,
Indeed is often stained with human "excrement".

Why God chooses thus to do I cannot tell,
Except that he may think it well
To show his power in a broken shell
That can no longer with his "echoes" swell.

To lift it up, and mend it, is His great delight,
To fill it once again with sounds of angel's flight,
So those who hold it to their ear might
Hear the Father speaking close and near.

Such healing mercy is the work of grace,
To take a broken one and then erase
The work of Satan, putting in its place
The image of His love -- the image of the Father's face.

Only One has come in human form
Who did not leave that form more torn
Than when He took it, being born
Of earth, and thus of heaven shorn.

And being found in human form
He chose to bear our sin and scorn,
Letting His own perfect flesh be torn
So ours could be redeemed – re-born.

And now, He welcomes those who come to him
With brokenness; asking him mend
And fill their shattered shells again
So they can be the holy gifts that He intends?

A Sunday Morning Poem

Sunday mornings are a mix of things
And among them all, the choir sings.
I love the thoughts the preacher brings
But mostly I'm glad the choir sings.
Whether we're good or floundering,
Cheryl smiles, encouraging,
And lifts us up on music's wings,
To praise our God
        each time the choir sings.

Morning Hope

Morning brings a hope with it
In which all human aspirations sit;
A hope that as the sun is rising,
So shall we, by God's devising;
Ever more to live and gaze upon
Life Giver, and Life Giver's Son.

The Goal, The Way, and The Key

*If anyone would come after me, he must deny himself
And take up his cross daily and follow me. For whoever
wants to save his life will lose it, but whoever loses his
life for me will save it. Luke 9: 23, 24*

Life is the goal,
   the promise,
      the everlasting hope.
Life free and whole,
   eternal, like His,
      is that to which we grope.

Death is the way,
   clearing our paths
      of mortal debris,
His death? Nay!
   "Our deaths", He laughs,
      "In death, it is 'we'!
         I died for you, now
            you must die for me."

Faith is the key;
   against all doubt,
      He trusted God;
And we trust that He,
   will someday, with a shout,
      make immortal,
         our mortality.

A prayer For A Glorious Day

May the sun shine on your way,
Delight your eye and bid you stay
To see the beauty of each glorious ray -
Then will your heart rejoice and say,
"This is indeed a God-made day!"

Good Morning Sunshine

Morning is rich with its promise of joy,
Golden with brightness to buoy
The spirit that craves an alloy
To strengthen its will and shadows destroy.

Come golden morning and lighten my way.
Come golden orb, to warm me - then stay,
So my verdict will be at the end of the day,
"Thank God for gifts that lighten, not weigh."

A Triangle of Love

House
Builders know
A triangular truss
Can bear the snow,
And justify the trust,
Of those living below.

Two points, set far apart,
Supported by one aloft,
Each bearing their part,
United by stringers across.

Two hearts can work as one,
United by Love's point above,
Reaching across the distance,
Creating strength, by actions done
While trussed in a triangle of love.

Preciousness

"Precious", AHD tells me,
comes from the Latin and
has to do with "price".
I know, Lord, that the things I receive
from Your dear hand
and heart suffice . . . no,
go far beyond, and
far above mere price
into a realm where
cash is meaningless,
where only love can tell
what words would vainly

seek to say,
where love alone is currency
with which a debt of love to pay.

(AHD is The American Heritage Dictionary)

The Voice of God
(A long and tortured musing)

"God told me such and such."
I've heard, a hundred times, as much,
from those I judged sincerely touched;
for whose credentials I would vouch.

And even just last night,
I read in Isaiah,
where Sennacherib came to fight,
and said to Hezekiah,
"Jehovah Himself told me
to march against this country
and destroy it."

And yet I'm never sure I really know
just what that language means.
Few, I think, would have me go
as far as to assume they've seen
some thing that clearly shows,
or heard a voice to let them know,
the will of God . . .

Sennacherib, no doubt,
consulted the entrails of a sheep,
or asked his wise advisors about
the most propitious time to leap
upon his prey . . .

But what are we to think or say,
who face such claims
of Divine knowledge?
Are we to give the farm away?
Thank God old Hezekiah
found another way.

I'm left to assume I know,
or at least that I should know.
And so I say within,
"She has a *sense* that this is so,"
or perhaps again,
"He *feels* that God would have him go."

But often God is quoted clearly,
speaking friend to friend,
confidentially and dearly.
"Jim," He says, "I want to send
you blessings, late and early."

Then, at least, may I assume
a voice was heard,
speaking clearly to illume
the hearer, with a word
too personal to subsume;
a real . . . a spoken word?

What does it mean to say,
"God told me so!"?
And how can one convey,
so another soul can know,
the extraordinary way
God's love - God's word -
has filled one's soul?

God has spoken many ways;
not always as thunder,
not always as the earth quake,
sometimes in the still small voice.

He has "thundered" from heaven
in a voice that only one or two
could understand.
To all the others
it was only noise . . .
a clap of thunder
from His hand.

Sometimes the "hearers" merely say,
"It seems good to the Holy Spirit and to us"
to speak or act a certain way.
Sometimes God has spoken
through prophets
and preachers
and others who see;
through the mouths of babes,
an unbelieving High Priest,
or a poor, beleaguered donkey.
Sometimes he has come
in a vision or dream;
sometimes as an angel,
or a beggar . . .
a stranger who seems
no different, in essence,
from the regular stream.

How do I know all of this?
The Bible tells me so.
But it does not always tell me

how God spoke to holy men of old.
And there again I'm left to know -
to assume I know -
the manner in which He chose
to speak to Adam
to Noah
to Abram
to Moses.

Did it *seem* to them
that God had spoken?
Did they *sense*
that God would have them
say, or do, or go?
They seem to know.
Their actions seem to say,
"I know!"

Ah, Father! I know you hear me,
but am I hearing you?
Is every breath your breath?
Does each inspiration
come from you?
Are my words
Your words, incarnate?
If it is true that, in you,
I live and breathe
and have my being,
then it must be true
that every word I think or speak
is coming straight from you.

Ah, no. That cannot be.
Peter's words, you said,
were Satan's words;

well intended,
fervently spoken,
thought to be true,
but . . . Satan's words.

So when can I say,
with the confidence of Isaiah,
or Sennacherib
or Peter,
"God told me so!"?
Perhaps it is given to some,
such to say.
And perhaps some day,
in a clearly audible way,
You'll speak to me.
But until then, Lord,
I'm more comfortable saying,
"It *seems* good to the Holy Spirit,
and to me."

Loose Ends

Dear Lord,
I'm at loose ends,
a phrase my mother used
when her day ended
with chores undone,
or worse, less done
than when
her day began.

You, Lord, are the windlass
of the ship my
cargo fares in, and

the anchor that tells it
when to go
and when to stay.
I need Your weight
at both ends of all I do
so I'll not wander
aimlessly -
loose endedly.

Looking on the Bright Side

Gloomy days?

There are none;
   only days
   in which the sun
   hides its ways,
   as it, today,
   has done.

Gloomy is as gloomy does.

Gloomy is a state of mind;
   a blindedness
   that seeks to find
   a place to rest
   within this heart of mine
   on sunless days.

All days can be hope-full days!

Perfect Imperfection   Heart's Ease: The Home of Heart

Hope, undaunted by the shroud,
   imagines blue,
   and sings aloud
   a song it knew
   before the clouds
   o're spread the day.

Rumors of Eden

Eden is where it all began and Eden is where we expect it all will end. That is the Christian hope based on a faith that God, in Christ, is redeeming what was lost in that tragic fall. We feel the loss in our world; in our environment, our government – or lack of government, our culture, our relationships, and most especially in our bodies. Rumors of Eden past and Eden to come feed our hopes and our faith. What was lost can be restored, in part now, and fully at a future day when Eden becomes New Jerusalem. Just as we don't know the "nuts and fruits" of Eden, neither do we know what the "furniture" of that renewed Eden will be, but something in us will not let go our hope for it.

All who have that hope in them actively share it with the coming generations. They shape their lives by that hope, and work to bring its fruits to maturity in their lives and in their world. My desire is that my children and grandchildren will keep the hope alive in their hearts and in the choices they make in life.

These poems are dedicated to: Christopher and Allison; Aaron, Isaac, and Jacob; Joseph Michael; great granddaughter Kylie, and all who are yet to come.

Phenomena
(Meditations on a word)

I like phenomena much more than miracles;
They make no judgment of the *why* or *how* of things,
But simply make one wonder; stand in awe.

Phenomena are gentlemen and lay no obstacle –
Assess no blame – to those who choose to cling
To mundane explanations of the things they heard or saw.

Beacons they are, and banners, calling us to see;
But never telling what to think or do or say;
Calling without words, speaking without tongue.

They turn our head – command our gaze – but leave us free
To call them ordinary – plain events of every day;
Leave us free to live as though their song was never sung.

Phenomena are not rare events, though some,
Who see them rarely, would have us think it so.
Phenomena are like the air we breathe, as close as skin.

They require a prism to show us that they've come,
A gateway to our senses that will let us see and know
That we are in the presence of a Gift – that God has come again.

Note: phenomenon is from the Greek root, *phos*, meaning light.

Pleasure Seeking

This heart of mine is a perilous gift.
My brothers, the beasts,
I assume, are not "gifted" with this

Veritable feast
Of emotions that buffet and lift
My heart – and increase
Its penchant to drift.

Its penchant – every pleasure to know –
Is perverse; a thing of the will.
Lord, make my heart a place where I may go
To find loves that are lasting – loves that fill
This weak vessel, with pleasure – eternally so.
Pleasure that time cannot kill,
But rather, eternally grow.

I Must Go
(A Song)
(Words by Jim Rapp & Cheryl Brandt, music by Cheryl Brandt)

The King of Infinity came to occupy a place,
The Lord of Eternity entered into Time and Space,
The Son of Heaven's purity – born to a fallen race.
Hear him tell His Father, "I must go."

"I must go, I must go,
To Bethlehem I'll go, a world is dying there
And my love can heal it of its sin and pain,
To Bethlehem I'll go, to a dying world."

The Son of Consolation, bringing hope to those who weep,
The Shepherd of the flock seeking lost and dying sheep,
The Everlasting Fountain giving water from the deep,
Hear Him say to His disciples, "I must go."

"I must go, I must go,
To Samaria I'll go, a heart is thirsting there

And my love can fill her empty yearning soul,
To Samaria I'll go, to a thirsting soul."

The ever present Savior seeks the farthest lonely hill,
Knowing death awaits Him, ever pressing onward still,
The Guiltless for the guilty, robbing Satan of a kill,
Hear His lonely words, "I must go."

"I must go, I must go,
To Jerusalem I'll go, a man is dying there
And my love can save him in his final hour,
To Jerusalem I'll go, to a dying man."

If you make your bed in hell,
Say to the darkness, "Cover me!"
If you take wing to flee from Him
Still you'll hear Him say,
"I must go, I must go,
You can not flee so far from me
That I'll not seek you there,
And my love can reach you in your sin and pain,
I must go,
Love compels,
I must go."   (repeat)

A Child's Gift of Love

A child offered me a morsel of his food
To share because he thought it good
And wanted me to know just where I stood
Within his range of values. And I should
Give him back, from my own store,
The equal of his gift and more.
My impulse is, from pockets full, to pour

Out worthless coins . . .
    God help me give him more.

Defining Beauty

How to define a beauty that the eyes cannot see;
Beauty of heart, beauty of mind, beauty of spirit;
Beauties that reflect what's dwelling inwardly.

Heart beauty is a beauty of openness,
Receptiveness of all who come to it,
Tender, receiving, enfolding, enriching-ness.

Mind beauty is keen, quick, incisive,
Filled with wisdom, practicality and wit,
Sure of self but not, of other's lights, dismissive.

Spirit beauty is most beautiful of all,
Heaven breathed, heaven-lit,
It knows when to bow and to stand tall.

The Teacher's Burden

The burden of a teacher is
To fairly judge the student's work;
To help him own its faults as his;
To own his duty, and to never shirk.
But what when one seems not to shirk,
But ineffectually to strive
For excellence, and do his work?
How then to make his spirit thrive;
To give him needed help
But keep his hope alive?
That is the burden of a teacher.

The Longing of A Human Heart

Good things always have a sad ending.
It's inevitable I think
Since everything we touch is tending
Toward decay,
A simple blink
And something precious,
Like a vapor, fades away.
I'd like to think that there are ways
To keep the gladness of our days,
To forestall the evening sun,
Or to call again the face of one
Who's long been gone away.
I want to think that there are things
That do not flee
But come again on golden wings
So we can see
Their beauty,
Feel their warmth,
Know their joy,
And once again, enfolded be;
Enfolded in their goodness
Everlastingly.

A Lament At the End of the Day

A busy day is like a band of thieves;
It robs us of our hours
And often leaves
Us struggling, with weakened powers,
To achieve,
In moments, what should be given hours.

Waking Thoughts

What does waking feel like?
I've watched a child awake
And smile as though the little tyke
Had every thirst of living slaked.

Oh that each waking might so be;
That every sleeper, waking, find that she,
Or he, had eased the burden he,
Or she, had carried into sleep so recently.

Something

There is a "something" in awaking
From a long and satisfying rest;
Something cozily enfolding.
Akin, it is, to taking
Some loved thing into your breast
For gentle, loving holding.

The Worth of a Touch

How much is a touch worth?
How much at a baby's birth?
At moments of sorrow;
    at moments of mirth?
More than the wealth of the earth!

Shadowed Blessings
*(Commemorating a shadow-frame
around a photo of a loved one)*

The sun found its way
Through the east-shading trees
And cast it rays
Across the stairway wall, intending thus to please
My eyes today.

The shadows formed
Were images of the rail along the steps
And they transformed
My way into a mystic passage, swept
With memories of the past re-formed.

For in their grace,
They circled there, for me to valuate,
A lovely face
Of one whose memory, accentuate,
My heart desires to daily trace.

Tell me not
That shadows bear no good to us;
The joy I've got,
Today alone, is proof enough
That shadows can be blessing-fraught.

Sin

Hurry is a sin.
It takes the fatness of God's love,
And makes it thin.

A Lament for Atheists

How sad when great minds –
Images of the Omniscient One –
Stumble at the thought of God.

I search their words and hope to find,
A tiny flash of faith among
The gloom they spread abroad.

Made with His features fine,
Their minds with His sinews strung,
Yet shrouded, they are, by dark doubt's hood.

Atheist! Even in negation they find
That the name they've unwittingly flung
At the world contains His Name, dimly understood.

Friendship

I can't see things the way you do;
Our angle of vision is not the same;
Our points of reference
   were set in different eras;
We form our definitions
   using different lexicons;
And, yes, our DNA,
   our daily living,
   our past and our present
   conspire to separate us.

So how can we be friends,
   not seeing the same things
   in the same way?

Friends reveal themselves
   with words like:
      "When I was young . . ."
      "Where I come from . . ."
      "My family always . . ."
      "I used to think . . .
         or feel . . .
         or wish . . ."

Or explain themselves, saying:
   "I meant to say . . ."
   "I get nervous when . . ."
   "That makes me feel so good."
   "I dream that someday . . ."
   "Oh, that makes me very sad."

Or seek to know, asking:
   "Why do you . . .?"
   "How can I . . .?"
   "When could we . . .?"

Friends have always known,
   about "damaged" genes
   and "dysfunctional" families,

Known that friendship is the cure
   for wounded egos
   and imperfect pasts,

Known that God himself
   never loved us more
   than when he saw us broken.

Perfect Imperfection

I can't see things the way you do;
Our angle of vision is not the same;
Our points of reference
 were set in different eras;
We form our definitions
 using different lexicons;
Our DNA,
 our daily living,
 our past and our present
 conspire to separate us.

So how can we be friends?

Friends allow each other in,
Saying, "Here! Stand were I stand,
 you'll see what I see."

Friends are prisms, bending light until,
 what they see, and feel, and are,
 fills the eye, the heart, the mind,
 of one they hope to call their friend.

A Malleable Moment

Every moment –
Momentous or not –
Deemed minute
Or even minuscule –
Is a gift as big as the world,
Holding in its fragile hand
All the possibilities available
To our time-bound race.

Though our minds can remember
Moments past,
And our "hearts" dream
Of moments to come,
It is this present moment –
This one instant
In which we live –
That is malleable to our will.

Rumors of Eden

In that once lush crescent that runs
From Egypt north to the Euphrates
Then slowly turns
To wind its way with downhill ease
Toward the Ancient ruins of Ur
Are found the roots, we're told,
The stock, from which our
Fathers built an ancient store that holds
The building blocks of all we know;
The DNA of man and beast
And every plant that grows
From greatest to the least.

And those who wander from that Eden,
Every man, or plant, or beast, transplanted,
Find their vital force disburdened,
Weakened in a foreign soil explanted.
And so with every passing generation
The cultivars that from that garden rose,
Growing fainter, cease to pass along
The ancient strains from which Edenic gardens grow.
Oh that we could scale the fence and breach the wall,
Evade the flaming sword that's set to guard that store!

With Eden's pristine stock we could reverse the fall,
Renew our world and live forevermore.

There are rumors that, in hidden places,
Edenic apples grow, and aboriginal creatures roam.
If we could find them, snatch their DNAs,
Then we could fix our damaged chromosomes.
But where to find that Eden?
And how to pass the flaming sword?
And how to know that, even then,
Our skills could reunite the broken cords?
There is a rumor that Eden has been breached,
That One has passed the Flaming Angel
And, the vial of life, has reached.
That rumor is our only hope – the great evangel!

Because You Asked
(A poem-response to a question)

You asked - or wondered at -
The meaning of happiness. You guessed
Quite rightly of its roots; that
Happiness - gay Happiness - when pressed
Admits her "joy" is made of happenings;
Of things, and moods, and times
That pass away.

Her sister, Joy - less often sought,
Because she can't be found by seeking -
Her sources twain, and naught
But twain can bring her into being -
Comes only when the *seeing eye* beholds
The *giving Hand*, responds with Joy,
And then rejoices.

Last Thoughts

What is the purpose of that last thought;
That last remembering of things I ought
To do when I get home at night?
Why did I have that "dream" of possibilities,
Of ways to strengthen my abilities
To do the things I do more right?
Why all this planning if, at this very moment,
I come face to face with death's certain omen,
And then cease forever to see light?

What can the purpose be –
       except there be Eternity?

Time-Tied

The words that end the day
Must bear the weight of all that we would want to say
If given all the night, and then could find a way
To put in words the things that heavy lay
Upon our hearts; the things that often play
Around the fringes of our talk and may,
At times, slip in a while. but later go away
To be forever lost, or wait some distant day,
Perchance, when with their kin-thoughts they
Will come again and find that time has gone away;
Replaced forever by eternal day;
That time has been unshackled, and that in that newer day
All thoughts will have full hearing - all things we wished to say
Will find expression in some word, or in some other way.

Recognizing God's Goodness

Oh God, Is time a gift? I know it is the only way
That you could give me life, so when you lay
Upon my feeble frame another hour, I hear you say,
"Child, this is a gift I give to show my love today.
You may grumble at its weight, or use it in some way
That brings you pleasure from another bygone day."

A Cup of Warm

I'd love to share a cup of warm with you,
But you are *there* and there is little I can do
But sit *here*, staring at the steam that rises to
Remind me that, despite the miles,
    When *here* . . . and *there*,
        Two cups are raised . . .
            One heart is made of two.

If I Could

If I could send you sunshine,
You'd never see a day
Without some hours of brightness
To whisk your cares away.
And If I had the power to do
The many, many things
I want to do for you,
You'd never lack for lack of joy;
You'd never lack for lack of peace;
You'd never lack for lack of hope;
You'd never lack for lack of love.
I'd fill your life,

And fill your heart,
And fill your future too,
With all the gold that one can know;
The gold that comes from knowing
God loves you.

On Being Perfect
(Be perfect as your Father
in heaven is perfect. Matt. 5:48)

From nothing, we are told,
God made all that we behold.
But is it really from nothing then;
Did it not all come from Him;
From His mind and from His thought?
But also from His Essence He has brought
To life another like Himself; a creature
Bearing eternity in its very nature.
Oh, that we would be, like He,
Perfect, so that we, like He
Could, from our treasure store,
Draw gifts that, given,
        last and bless forever more.

Troubled Waters

Imagine how stale would be
The waters of the world
If there were no movement;
No churning of the sea,
No rushing of the brook,
No rising of the tide.
Imagine how stagnant

It would be,
And how the beauty that we see
In falling waters
Would be lost.
Regretfully
We sometimes curse the things
God meant to be
A blessing.
Oh friend, let you and me
Rejoice each time we see His hand,
The Hand of Him
Who freshness loves,
Revealed in "troubled" waters;
"Troubled" for good of you and me.

Wednesdays Ending

Wednesdays ending
Are heart rending,
Grandsons sending,
Sadness blending
Days.

Lord of every day,
Make the things I say,
And make the way
I say them, play
A role someway;
To sway
Their hearts so they
Will say,
"Here Lord, today,
And every other day,
I'll walk your way."

Not Hearing Less

Words! Imperfect conductors!
Gifts from God!
But, in human hands -
On human tongues -
From human hearts,
And human minds -
They may convey to others
Something other than intended.

I've seen a love-struck fool
Convinced that "drop dead!",
From one he admires -
Though spoken with utter disdain -
Was actually meant to mean,
"You are a drop-dead,
Good looking man
I'd love to take to bed with me."

Or there are those I've known
Whose blighted minds
Insist on parsing words so finely
That they cannot hear,
Or "see", or "feel"
The intensity of true love
With which their "lover"
Would invest them.

The words are blameless,
Mere carriers, caring not
From whom, to whom, or what
They're asked to bear.
In the end it is the hearing ear,
The receiving heart,

That shapes their destiny, making of them
Words that fan a flame or cool a fire.

Ah, Friend, I cannot know for sure,
The meaning of the words you say,
I may, as all frail humans may,
Hear more or less in them
Than you intended to convey.
May I err on the side of generosity,
Hearing more of good, more of love,
Less of hurtful intentionality.

Love Is Not Blind

Love is not blind.
Something like love,
Something some call love,
May induce one to choose
Not to see,
But "choosing" not to see
Is not "not seeing";
It is denial
Of what one sees,
Hoping what is seen is ephemeral –
Will not last –
Or will in time
Be morphed into something else,
Something wished for,
Something more love-worthy
Than what it knows to be.
And in the end it accepts,
For as long as it can hold it,
A façade called love,
A thin shell filled with delusion

Desire and disappointment.
Nothing more.

No, Love sees.
It does not deny –
Does not excuse –
What it sees,
But loves anyway,
Wishing for perfection
In what it loves –
Not for its own pleasure
But for the good of the one loved –
But does not insist upon it
As a condition of its favor.

Love never ceases
To long for the time
When truth meets truth,
Faithfulness meets faithfulness,
Love meets love.
Though it is crushed, reviled,
And rejected, it prays,
"Forgive them,
For they don't know what they are doing."

Daring a Correction

Madeleine L'Engle quotes H.A. Williams,
"The opposite of sin can only be faith,
    and never virtue."
I like that, but would change it slightly,
"The *alternative* to sin can only be faith,
    and never virtue."

Four Healings

And they brought their sick to Him . . .

One He sent on his way, saying,
"Go, your body is healing itself."

Another He sent to the physicians, saying,
"I have taught them how to heal you."

To still another He said, "I will heal you,
be made clean and whole."

And to the last He said, "Today,
you will be with me in Paradise."

. . . and He healed them all.

A Prayer for Selflessness

I have grown too big, Lord . . .

Make me small enough to fill your heart.
Trim my ambitions to the size that fits your will;
My aspirations . . . let them be your breath; from start
To end, My goal, your heart to fill.

My heart is so full of me, Lord . . .

Make my swollen heart small enough
To fit in yours; To fill it as David's did -
"After your heart", made "in your image", not earthly stuff;
The "apple of your eye"; my heart, in your heart hid.

Make me small enough to live in your great heart . . .

Precious Gift of Life

(A poem sent to a friend after he had learned
he had terminal cancer.)

Life is a gift so precious –
So precious it cannot be weighed in our hand.
Weighed in our hand it would seem worthless;
Worthless – less even than dust or sand.

Life is a gift so precious –
So precious it cannot be measured in years.
Measured in years it will always be finite;
Finite – ended in sorrows and tears.

Life is a gift so precious –
So precious it must be given away.
Given away, it becomes eternal;
Eternal – weighed, measured –
Part of God's Eternal Day.

The Eternal Day

This day has started on another round,
And even in expressing that, I've found
An inconsistency that threatens fair
To catch my logic in its snare.

This day is, of course, a day unto itself,
Not an older one taken from the shelf
And sent around again to do
The things it should have done, anew.

This day must give account, to the great Chronologer,
For hours spent as busy saint or noisy roisterer.
But when, I wonder, did this day begin its round,
And where, I wonder, will its end be found?

Morning's Message

What is the best time of day?
Morning is a lovely time to say,
"I wish for you, my friend, a perfect day;
A day whose moments bring good things to lay
Before you, giving you a marvelous array
Of choices." Morning is God's loving way
Of showing us His love has come to stay.
As surely as the Sun inscribes its way
Through heaven's paths, we hear Him say,
"I am eternal truth, eternal life, the everlasting way."

The Making of Ezer

When the sun was made, and brightly lit
God allowed that He was pleased with it.
And all the other things He made were "fit",
But in the last, the man, He saw a deficit.

And so he set himself to work again.
He took the man apart, and took from him,
A slender rib, and fashioned, there and then,
An Ezer, to be man's completion . . .
                  Man's companion-friend.

Seeking A Mate And Finding One's Self

Everything after it's own kind,
Each a doubled product of the Father's mind.
And each instructed to leave behind
Multiplied copies for others to find.

But in man's "original" it was not so;
A solitary figure sent to go
Throughout creation, yearning to know
An "other" through which his seed could flow.

Naming, but never claiming, he went,
And at day's end, weary and bent,
He curled himself around himself and sent
To his Maker a wordless cry . . . "I am alone, I'm spent!"

And the Maker of all that was good
Saw that his Image would,
If left to himself, self-destruct; he could
Not be left alone. It was *not* good.

Carefully incising from the original clay,
The Maker fashioned a Self in an opposite way,
And gave to His Image a mate that day;
"Self of my Self," the man said, "Clay of my clay."

"Go now, be one flesh!" the Maker decreed,
"And reflect, through your seed -
Through your Selves - My Image indeed,
Two Selves in one spirit agreed."

The Prayer of Hezekiah

Fifteen years is all I ask, Lord,
Fifteen more years to do your will!
"Granted," came the answer,
"Turn your head and weep no more."

The pundits say it ended badly,
that he should have been content
to live as long as God allowed,
and then to lay his life down gladly.

Perhaps the pundits know.
They make it their business to know,
and then to let us know they know.
But do they really know?

I've measured the value of fifteen years
and found them filled with Goldenness;
with Treasure I would now regret to lose,
though mixed, they've been, with many tears.

Trail's End

We only see the trail's end.
It is where we live, at trail's end.
Step by step,
Word by word,
Deed by deed,
We extend the trail
But ever and always
We stand at trail's end.

Fools believe that they can see,
Or step, or cast their lives
Beyond trail's end,
Not knowing that
Each plan,
Each hope,
Each effort
Only and always leaves them
Standing at trail's end.

No eye can see beyond,
No thought can comprehend,
No deed extend beyond
Trail's end.

The meaning of each life
Is in the trail that lies behind.
Lives loved,
Wounds bound up,
Hands extended,
Lessons taught,
Joys shared,
All follow,
And will stand with us,
Witnesses, forever and always,
At trail's end.

An Ode to Memory

There is only one road to travel,
The ever-unfolding, well-worn path called "now".

Standing on the high precipice
Of the eternal moment,

The unknown looms ahead,
A wispy, wishful construct, shaped to resemble
Cherished memories from the past.

The once-known, once-held, once-cherished
Lies behind us, muted mounds
Of all we've had, and said, and done.

As *now* crumbles
Under the weight of our mortality,
We cling to faith for this moment,
Hope for some tomorrow,
And draw comfort
From what used to be.

Memory -
        all that's left of everything.

On A Gloomy Morning

On a gloomy, gloomy morning
When the sun is hid from view,
And no lightness is aborning
To ignite the morning dew,
Turn your longing to the Brightness
That is new each dawning day;
He will fill your heart with light-ness
Driving all your cares away.

Continental Drift

In ages too distant for memory,
Some cosmic jolt created rifts;
Made two, or more,
Of that which once was One.

With slow inevitability
The jagged parts began to drift
Until the distance, shore to shore,
Erased all memory of the One.

But time, that stretches through eternity,
The mortal enemy of rifts,
When it will stretch no more,
Calls back, all drifters, to the One.

And with the same inevitability
The course and forces shift;
Allied, they guide and pull back to the core,
The wand'ring parts, and make them One.

A Divine Mystery

Theologians may argue the relative worth of our religious holidays but children instinctively turn to Christmas. One could cynically suggest that gifts are the reason for their delight but history indicates differently. Even in eras and in places where circumstances limited, or prevented, the giving of gifts, children were, and still are drawn to the manger where a baby lays. The baby is the gift.

I remember more than one Christmas when my brothers and I were given our "Christmas present" early, a new bathrobe replacing the previous outgrown one, which would become our "shepherd's robe" for the annual Christmas play. (I have no memory of any of us wearing our robes on any other occasion so they truly became *our* gift to the Christ child.)

It is appropriate that I dedicate this last section of poems to my siblings, only one of whom remains, with whom I celebrated so many joyous Christmas Days. To Istra, Marvin, and Donald I dedicate these poems.

Snowflakes

If snow flakes were made of love,
And I really think they are,
Being as much the product of
Our Father as His brightest star,
Then naturally they'd bear to us
The bounty of their maker's hand.
Coming in their ways ambagious,
Countless gifts of love descend.

A child will tell you what she knows
That makes the snow so precious;
Not with words, but in the joy she shows
As each flake blesses her with kisses.
Tender skin exposed to heaven's gifts,
Feels the coolness of their presence;
Feels the trickle of their meaning, and lifts
A praise of wordless essence.

The Father is always making gifts of love;
And some He sends in what we call a storm.
But He, with wisdom from above,
Knows that snowflakes, to a child, are warm --
Reminders, they, of a Father's gentle care --
And cause the child to turn her face,
In joyful thanks, and bless the stormy air
That brings reminders of her Father's grace.

An Old-fashioned Christmas

Things haven't changed much
Since the wise men loaded their "trucks"
And started out in search of a king.

They needed a special light
To guide them at night
Past distractions and dangers enough
To discourage any but a serious seeker.

There are lights aplenty today
Proclaiming a glad holiday,
But only the wise find the way.

Past distractions and dangers
The light-led still come to the manger,
And mingle their wonder
With shepherds and angels
In the old-fashioned way

Mary and Joseph in the Shadowlands
(Song Lyrics)

We thought we could leave the shadows behind;
Sneers, and whispers, and words unkind;
Condemnation for this choice of mine.
Those shadows we thought we could leave behind.

Oh, Father of lights
Can it really be true
That this child is Your Son,
That you've sent Him to do
What prophets foretold,
And ancients desired –
Make a way through the darkness
And shadowy mire?

But shadows were part of the journey that day;
Shadows of doubt on my mind would play;
Over-shadowed was I, as the angel did say;

Perfect Imperfection   A Divine Mystery

So walking through shadows we found our way.

Oh, Father of lights
Can it really be true
That this child is Your Son,
That you've sent Him to do
What prophets foretold,
And ancients desired –
Be light in the darkness
And shadows retire?

Bethlehem lies at the foot of the hill;
Quietly shadowed, sleeping and still.
Look up darkened souls, the Son of Desire
Will shadows dissolve, in the light of His fire.

Oh, Father of lights
Can it really be true
That this child is Your Son,
That you've sent Him to do
What prophets foretold,
And ancients desired –
To scatter the darkness
As shadows expire?

Oh, Father of lights
It really is true
That this child is Your Son,
That you've sent Him to do
What prophets foretold,
And ancients desired –
To scatter the darkness –
To scatter the darkness –
To scatter the darkness –
As shadows expire?

One Clear Star

One clear star, one clear light,
To pierce the darkness of the night,
To pierce the darkness of the night,
And bathe a stable in its light.

One tiny Child; whose Infant's might
Would crush the foe of all that's right,
Would crush the foe of all that's right
And build a kingdom by His might.

One choice to make, one single choice,
To join His cause and lift one's voice,
To join His cause and lift one's voice,
Or turn away - reject the choice.

One clear choice, one last ray,
One fateful chance to turn and say . . .
One fateful chance to turn and say,
"Come, cleansing light" . . . "Come, heaven's ray".

The Peace Maker

How dare they speak to us
      of peace on earth,
This triple decimated band,
      survivors of that cosmic war
      that tore the heavens
      and desecrated earth.

Perfect Imperfection A Divine Mystery

Are we to believe our
      shattered world,
Triple torn by
      selfishness, greed and arrogance,
      can be redeemed
      by one Child's birth?

Or do they know
      what we must learn,
That He alone, who healed their broken realm,
      restoring peace in heaven,
      can heal our stubborn hurts
      and bring us peace on earth?

A Child's Way

A smile blessed me today.
Without knowing she had done so,
a child's smile at her friend,
in an unassuming way,
caught my heart, mid-beat,
and sent me singing through the day.
Yes, peace on earth can come,
but only in a child's way.

The Postage Is So High

Each year we face the task
Of culling names from
Our Christmas mailing list.
And so I duly ask,
"Is this one dead, or just at risk?
Have the Jones moved?

Did Eddy send a card last year?
Should we mail to everyone
Or not to those who live quite near?"
All are questions that must be asked.
But then there's the cost of mailing.
Being old, I remember mailings past
That cost, in whole, a simple shilling,
A mere three cents apiece.
Now one stamp alone exceeds
Four-tenths the total Christmas budget
Dad, in childhood, ceded me.
I wonder, did my father begrudge it?
Or did another Father, sending Gifts,
Regret the cost to Him?
I think, on further contemplation
I'll gladly mail our "cards",
Without consideration of the cost,
To all our priceless friends again.

He Didn't Come To Be A Star

He didn't come to be a star;
To hobnob with the world's elite.
He came to find us where we are;
To live and walk earth's humble streets.
He didn't seek the world's acclaim
Nor come to fan rebellion's fire –
To build a kingdom, make a name –
He didn't come to be a star.

Incarnated in a baby's frame,
The Son of God – whose very name
Bespoke a faithful servant's claim,
Whose only hope, whose joy of gain,

Was mixed with Calvary's pain –
Became a man and once again
Hope sprang! And now the ugly stain
Is washed away by Calvary's crimson rain.

Walking as a man among us,
Tested like a man in every way,
Feeling, like a man, the evil malice,
Of the one who holds strong sway.
Giving all his humble service,
Daily pouring out his soul in prayer
That the Father's love would save us
And return us to His care.

Announced by angels from afar,
Still, He didn't come to be a star.

One Clear Star
(With suggestions from Cheryl Brandt)

Lord, You chose a star
To direct the Wise Men to the Savior.
Why should a thing without a voice
Be given such a favor?
What made a heavenly light your choice?

Maker of all things,
Is there a part of all creation
You did not employ
To announce, with grandest acclamation,
Your Divine envoy?

Perfect Imperfection   A Divine Mystery

We are told that
Those in darkness saw the light
With a brilliance surging;
That they ventured through the night
At the heavenly beacon's urging.

And the host of Angels sang –
A light-enshrouded throng –
Drawing from the past
Words they'd practiced for so long.
They sang of hope, and light, and life at last.

The shepherds, lazing in the fields –
Until their tongues were set aflame
By the burnished messengers who came
To tell them where the child was lain –
Could not help but spread his fame.

And even beasts
Of every kind and nature,
Standing 'neath that telling light,
Must have seen in it, Your signature;
Seen, and gladly owned their Maker's right.

This Is Christmas

Snow covered houses and snow-laden streets,
Lights in the windows and strung from the eaves,
Elves and reindeer carrying treats,
Signal it's time for families to meet.

The kitchen, dispensing its chatter and smell,
Sends through the house a message to tell
Everyone present at Gramma's "hotel",
"A feast is coming . . . your tummy to fill!"

Aunts, and uncles, and cousins arrive
With arm-loads of presents, trying to hide
What children, with bright prying eyes,
Imagine they carry in tinseled disguise.

This we call Christmas, our premier celebration;
A time to reconnect what time's separation
Has severed; a re-consecration
Of valued and sacred relations.

Reminiscent, it is, of the first Christmas Day,
When, with lights, and singing, and giving away
Of the best that He had, our Father would say,
"I send peace, wrapped in flesh, to the world today."

A Divine Mystery

It is June today . . . almost July,
And I am thinking of a winter sky
When snow clouds will be flying by,
And wondering . . . asking why
A snowflake, citizen of heaven high,
Would choose to come to earth to die.

It could be love that drew it nigh;
Love, inspired by earth-kind's thirsty sigh;
A love that ever longs to water what is dry.

Perfect Imperfection   A Divine Mystery

Perfect Imperfection

Alphabetical List of Poems

A "Song" for Bud & Pat 66
A Birthday Blessing 74
A Child's Gift of Love 169
A Child's Way 201
A Cup of Warm II 73
A Cup of Warm 180
A Defining Issue: What is Pentecostal? 111
A Divine Mystery 205
A Final Word 120
A Grain of Mustard Seed 150
A Hill Far-away 97
A Hymn 139
A Joy Worth Waking For 35
A Lament at the End of the Day 171
A Lament for Atheists 174
A Little Comfort For An Untidy Man 22
A Malleable Moment 176
A Mother's Day Poem for My Wife 62
A Pastor 76
A Path to Joy 149
A Patriot's Prayer and a Response 100
A Play Without A Script 19
A Prayer for a Glorious Day 156
A Prayer for Friday, February 11, 2005 140
A Prayer for June 3, 2005 136
A Prayer For My Neighbor 95
A Prayer For Peace 88
A Prayer for Selflessness 186
A Prayer 148
A Resolution From A Very Wordy Man 54
A Sabbath Remembered 23
A Samaritan Leper's Song 142

A Sea-sick Mariner's Lament 21
A Seminal Question 12
A Sunday Morning Poem 154
A Sunday Morning Prayer 145
A Triangle of Love 157
A Valentine Poem 67
A Valentine's Day Poem 68
A Valentine's Day Prayer 68
A Weatherman's Lot Is Not A Happy One 13
A Wish For Joy 76
A Work Deferred For Lack of Purity 85
Ahasuerus's Sin 100
An Eye Opener 40
An Invitation to Dance: Declined 39
An Ode to Memory 191
An Ode To Three Wonderful Boys 64
An Old-fashioned Christmas 197
As You Have Said, Let It Be Unto Me 55
Astigmatism 17
At the End of the World 109
Autonomy: To Be Or Not To Be 11
Balaam's Speaking Ass 98
Because You Asked 178
Close Pleasures 6
Come Lord 146
Come! Enjoy the Moon! 34
Concentrated Light 47
Congenital Twins 12
Consistency 13
Continental Drift 193
Countless Shades 96
Daring a Correction 185
Defining Beauty 170
Ducky Days 15
Eclipsed 38

Faithful Luna..33
Father of fathers 71
For A Nurse-Friend Watching Her Father Die......................69
Forgiveness 122
Four Healings..186
Four Words 144
Friendship 174
Good Morning Sunshine 156
Good Morning! 143
Grace..153
He Didn't Come To Be A Star..202
Heart Work...47
Heart's Ease: The Home of Heart 136
Heel Pullers..94
Honor 61
How Will We Praise Him?..145
I Must Go 168
I'll Rise on His Love..134
If I Could..180
Images..127
In All Things Give Thanks...144
In Memoriam 61
In Memory of Sylvia – A Dear Friend 71
Incorrectly Rectal..19
Introspection 49
Jehovah-Rapha..117
Justice..88
Last Thoughts...179
Less Les 27
Let Everything That Hath Breath Praise Him 147
Living In The Shadow of a Shadow.................................90
Looking on the Bright Side 163
Loose Ends...162
Love By Demolition...101
Love Is Not Blind..184

Luna and Sol	37
Luna on a Cold, Cold, Night	34
Luna	33
Making Mud Into Moonlight	39
Martha's Complaint	148
Mary and Joseph in the Shadowlands	198
Me and God (And Some Farmer)	3
Men Who Know What They Know	99
Mixed Economies	104
More Questions Than Time Allows	92
Morning Hope	155
Morning's Message	188
Morning's Soft Light	133
Mortality	95
Naked Reflection	36
Name Bearers	113
No Animals Died	26
Not Hearing Less	183
Not My Words, But Thine	46
Of Shepherds and Sheep	106
On A Gloomy Morning	192
On Being Perfect	181
On Being Right	105
On Democracy	119
On Faithfulness	91
On Loving (or not) The Wrinkles	79
On Naming	14
On Reviewing My Poetry	57
On Sources of Inspiration	51
One Clear Star	200
One Clear Star	203
Our Luna Friend	34
Parallel Lives: Inversely Related	125
Patience	146
Pentecost	125

Perfect Imperfection	45
Period . . . *italicized*	16
Phenomena	167
Planning for the Future	20
Pleasure Seeking	167
Praise	53
Precious Gift of Life	187
Preciousness	157
Psalm 99	134
Rain	5
Recognizing God's Goodness	180
Redemption	128
Righteousness	91
Rumors of Eden	177
Seeing the World	7
Seeking A Mate And Finding One's Self	189
Shadowed Blessings	173
Sharing Joy	135
Sin	173
Snowflakes	197
Sol Rising	41
Some Things I'd Rather Not Know	28
Something	172
Spellbound	8
Storms	6
Sunday Graces	145
Sunday Morning "Him" Singing	136
Superlatives	24
Supernova (The Lonely Center)	102
Tea-peed	12
Thank You, Ruth and Arlene	72
The "Story" of Dan	75
The Best Use Of The Best Words	48
The Danger of "Knowing" The Truth	87
The Eternal Day	187

The Gift of Time	147
The Goal, The Way, and the Key	155
The Longest Word	11
The Making of Ezer	188
The Matriculation of a Young Lady	70
The Meaning of Silence	52
The Mystery of Luminosity	38
The Parent's Tithe	21
The Peace Maker	200
The Perfect Day	141
The Poet's Sword	54
The Postage Is So High	201
The Prayer of Hezekiah	190
The Prophet's Eye	83
The Renaming of Jacob	77
The River From Lothlorien	22
The Servant's Prayer	137
The Storm	114
The Teacher's Burden	170
The Voice of God	158
The Worth of a Touch	172
Thinking About Man's Use of Time	87
This Is Christmas	204
This Is My Body	123
Thoughts About A M	4
Time-Tied	179
To Allison	74
Trail's End	190
Tricky Autumn	7
Troubled Waters	181
Truth Tellers	50
Truth	86
Twinkle Toes	18
Two Rocks	79
Unlinked Hours	25

Upon Being Appointed *Lever Laureate* 20
Voice to Voice 110
Waking Thoughts..172
Wednesdays Ending..182
What Is A Poem? 55
What is the Shape of Joy? 133
What Mean These Stones...65
What We Know About Friendship...62
Wonderful Memories 53
You Are Joy!...141

Perfect Imperfection

About The Author

James (Jim) Rapp is a retired public school teacher.

Previous to his 27 year teaching career he served as pastor of a congregation in River Falls, Wisconsin for six years. In the years since his retirement from teaching he served his church in Eau Claire, Wisconsin as Director of Drama for 12 years until May 2009.

Jim holds a Diploma in Theology from North Central Bible College (now North Central University) 1958, and a Master's Degree in History from University of Wisconsin-River Falls 1971, with his major area of interest being the Ancient Near East.

He has written seven dramas, five of which have been staged. In his twelve years as Director of Drama he co-directed, with Music Director, Cheryl Brandt, twenty-two adult musical dramas and nine children's musicals.

Jim is author of three additional books of poetry, *Sandals: The Journey of Abraham and Sarah and Hagar*, *Second Crop: More Poems by James D. Rapp*, and *Etcetera: An Eclectic Expression of Humors*.

He is also author of *Inga & Olaf: Modern Parables* and *Sermon on the Mount: Brief Meditations*.

Jim lives with Alice, his wife of 56 plus years, in Eau Claire, Wisconsin.

Perfect Imperfection

Perfect Imperfection

Perfect Imperfection

www.ingramcontent.com/pod-product-compliance
Lightning Source LLC
Chambersburg PA
CBHW071451040426
42444CB00008B/1297